VENICE TOUR GUIDE FOR 2024

A thorough guide to discovering Venice's undiscovered attractions, fascinating culture and hidden gems

Karen O. Cox

TABLE OF CONTENTS

INTRODUCTION

Greetings from Venice

This beautiful city in northern Italy is made up of more than 100 islands, many of which are connected by bridges and the biggest of which is crisscrossed by blue-green canals to assist the never-ending traffic—all of it floating. Venice was established in 421 AD and is situated on the Venetian lagoon, a sizable inlet on the Adriatic Sea. It was a strong maritime kingdom that controlled the spice trade from 1000 AD to about 1630 AD and was governed by a series of brutal Dukes, or Doges as they were known locally.

The Grand Canal's main roadway is lined with golden palaces and merchant villas, which reflect the city's enormous riches. The powerful's riches allowed them to decorate their palazzos, guild halls, and churches with works by the best Italian and foreign painters, including Titian, Carpaccio, Tintoretto, Veronese, and many more.

The memory of this civic benevolence is what still draws visitors who like art. The city has influenced more than just talented artists. Many authors, including Henry James, Thomas Mann, and Ernest Hemingway, who frequented Harry's Bar-Bellini's, fell in love with Venice.

Along with Rome, Pisa, Florence, and Siena, Venice is one of the top 5 tourist attractions in Italy, therefore it is often busy, especially during the summer. It is essential to have your mind set on how to handle them. The St. Mark's Basilica, with its bell tower (Campanile San Marco) and enormous pigeon-filled piazza (Piazza San Marco), is the top sight on your list of must-sees. A gondola trip up the Canale Grande (Grand Canal) is a must-do. Visit the Ducal Palace and cross the Ponte de Sospiri, often known as the Bridge of Sighs.

You will find that the city is filled with cafés, restaurants, and stores to satisfy every taste, every budget, and every hunger in its winding and intersecting lanes. If you take your time and just give into the city, you will love the location much more. However, be aware that the tourism business has an iron hold on the city and that it appears to affect everyone and everything. The volume of tourists only tends to decrease throughout the frigid winter months before picking back up in February with the celebration of the Carnivale. Regardless of their numbers, they do not seem to lessen "La Serenissima" — the Divine Republic — enduring, sultry, and wet attractiveness.

Our opinion is that spring or fall are the greatest times to visit Venice since there are fewer visitors around, the weather is more pleasant, and there are cool seaside breezes. You may appreciate the coolness of freezing breezes and mists whether you visit in the morning or the evening.

Venice is a labyrinth, so going on your own without a guide may be a lot of fun. The best approach to experience the "real" Venice is definitely to let yourself get "lost" in the little lanes. However, if you want a guide, the approximate cost for a "tour escort" who stays with customers for 8 hours would be 250 EUR, or 150 EUR for a half day. You will pay roughly 150 EUR for a two-hour tour of a museum with a local guide.

The municipal and regional administration has taken several beneficial steps as a result of the significance of tourism to the contemporary Venetian economy. Previously restricted to licensed boaters only, Venice's canals are now available to guests who want to rent and operate their vessels. The mysterious fire-damaged Fenice Theatre has been repaired and reopened. Most crucially, the Moses Damn, which will stop Aqua Alta from often flooding again, is now being built.

The Venetian lagoon's other islands are also receiving the gift of fresh life. For instance, Lazzaretto Vecchio, once a shelter for stray dogs, is now a sizable sports facility. Formerly a Benedictine monastery, the island of San Servolo today houses a center for foreign crafts, while San Clemente just inaugurated a luxurious high-end hotel whose pampered guests have the island to themselves.

Travelers and visitors who dress casually in the British or American fashion should be aware that the Mayor and Council have implemented "10 commandments" that govern "indecorous" behavior. If you break the law, you could have to pay a fine right away. Among the guidelines: Bikini tops and clothing that exposes the midriff are prohibited (even in June through August, when temperatures may easily exceed 25°C and humidity levels are oppressively high). Do not picnic on church steps or take a dip in a fountain.

Okay, so why not? If you treat Venice with respect, she will reward you with priceless memories that you will cherish forever.

CHAPTER 1

The Uprising and Decline of the Venetian Republic in A Short History of Venice

The history of Venice, a city famous for its canals, bridges, and maze-like lanes, is just as fascinating as its design. In the past, this city served as the capital of a Mediterranean empire, did you know that? Or that the USA's Founding Fathers were inspired by its system of government? Let's go through time and see the fascinating history of Venice.

A Snippet of Venice's Long History

Even though all routes may lead to Rome, it seems that the Romans passed by this marshy region of the Adriatic, where the island city of Venice is located. Venice stands distinctive among the main Italian cities, as noted by historian John Foot, not only because of its unusual physical location but also because it did not exist during the height of the Roman Empire.

But as we will see, Venice was established by Romans fleeing the unrest in the Western Roman Empire. Additionally, the city did swear allegiance to the Eastern Roman or Byzantine Empire during its formative years, according to researcher Thomas F. Madden. Since then, the city has expanded its influence—or, more precisely, raised its sails—to control the Mediterranean trade routes for centuries.

Venice had become one of Europe's major powers by the 12th century. The city was well-known for its enormous commerce networks, a distinctive aristocratic republic type of government, a bustling Renaissance-era artistic scene, and a strong military, as historian David Abulafia demonstrates. Venice earned the moniker "La Serenissima" ("The Most Serene") because of all these factors.

Venice ruled colonial lands throughout the Adriatic and the eastern Mediterranean for centuries, but it never expanded into the kind of enormous geographical empire that Ancient Rome did. Therefore, even though we often consider Venice to be a single Italian city, it has a considerably larger Mediterranean footprint. So let's board our gondola and go around Venice's history and canals together!

Venice's Founding (421 AD–1082 AD)

Myths Regarding the History of Venice

The creation of Venice is a fascinating fusion of reality and fantasy. According to historian Elizabeth Horodowich, the founding of the city is a fascinating fusion of fact and myth. One of the most persistent myths is that on March 25, 421 AD, at exactly noon, Roman consuls from Padua built Venice. Although this story is probably more fiction than reality, it is a tribute to the entrepreneurial drive of the Venetians since it says that their city's creation was so important that it had a specific appointment time.

A Refuge in Venice: The First Settlers

The Western Roman Empire was disintegrating, and the first residents in Venice were fleeing the unrest there. According to historian Roberto Cessi, these early residents started to build some kind of government when they chose Orso (Ursus) as the first Doge or Duke in 727. Due to its advantageous position and the fortitude of its people, Venice had developed into a distant outpost of the Byzantine Empire by the year 751.

Several intricate conditions that developed throughout the Western Roman Empire's demise led to the creation of Venice. At its height, in the year 117 CE, the Empire included all of Europe from Italy to the British Isles, as well as North Africa, Egypt, Mesopotamia, and Anatolia. However, by 285 CE, the Empire had expanded to such a size that it was no longer possible for Rome, which served as its capital, to rule over all of the provinces.

Emperor Diocletian split the empire in half, with the capital of the Eastern Empire being Byzantium (later Constantinople) and the capital of the Western Empire being Milan. Both portions were referred to as "The Roman Empire," but as time went on, the Eastern Roman Empire made Greek its official language and largely lost its Roman heritage. While the Western Empire faltered and eventually crumbled in 476 CE, the Eastern Empire prospered.

Political instability, the self-interest of the two halves, barbarian tribe invasions, governmental corruption, mercenary armies, an over-reliance on slave labor, extreme unemployment and inflation, and the rise of Christianity were just a few of the factors that contributed to the decline of the Western Roman Empire. Political instability was a result of the lack of unity between the Eastern and Western sections of the empire, which was made worse by government corruption, particularly among provincial officials who exploited their positions for personal benefit.

A particularly turbulent time, the Crisis of the Third Century (235-284 CE), saw the rise and fall of 20 emperors in little under 50 years. The 26 emperors who governed during the 250 years between Augustus and Alexander Severus stood in sharp contrast to this instability. The crisis highlighted the danger of Rome's dependence on a single emperor, whose demise would cause instability.

Many individuals sought safety in Venice's marshy lagoons as a result of these issues. The Germanic and Hun incursions into Roman territory were the main reason for the refugees' flight. Venice's watery surroundings provide a built-in barrier against these incursions. The immigrants eventually established villages on several islands in the lagoon, including Torcello, Murano, Burano, and Lido, to acclimate to their new surroundings. To provide their structures with solid foundations in the swampy land, they drove wooden pilings into it. These dispersed settlements eventually merged to become the metropolis of Venice. Fishermen and salt workers made up the bulk of the early Venetian population. They developed skills in shipbuilding and navigation as well, which helped Venice become the dominant naval power it is today. Despite their difficult surroundings, the Venetians were able to build a vibrant city that would ultimately grow to be one of the most important towns in all of Europe.

The emergence of a distinctive city: Venice's New Identity

Beginning in the early 800s, Venice started to define its character. Thomas F. Madden, a historian, claims that the Byzantine ruler of the region transferred to the fortified island of Rialto, which is now a part of modern-day Venice. This action marked a major turning point for the city, especially after Charlemagne and the Franks' expensive siege of Venice between 810 and 814 failed. This triumph enhanced Venice's reputation and prepared the way for its development as a strong city-state.

The remains of St. Mark the Evangelist were taken out of Alexandria, Egypt, by Venetian traders in 828. This incident, together with the transfer of a significant ecclesiastical office to Venice, strengthened the city's authority. The renowned winged lion, which stands in for St. Mark, became Venice's emblem, representing the city's expanding power and distinct personality.

The Middle Ages in Venice (1082–1297 AD)

Venice's Development: A Growing Power

By this time, the people of Venice had developed into real products of both the Adriatic Sea and the lagoon where the city's connecting islands are situated. By granting Venice important commercial rights in 1082, the Byzantine Emperor Alexius I Comnenus achieved his goal of securing Venetian naval help against the Normans in southern Italy. Venetian merchants had a substantial competitive edge over their rivals thanks to this deal that freed them from taxes across the whole Byzantine Empire. These advantages encouraged Venetian traders to pursue new trade routes. Over time, Venice rose to prominence in the Mediterranean and controlled the crucial salt trade.

The Historical Role of a City: Venice and the Crusades

Venetian-Byzantine ties, however, began to deteriorate by the late 1170s. The emperor encouraged competitors of Venice, like Genoa, to do business in Byzantine marketplaces. Despite a brief improvement in ties, Venetians' animosity against the Byzantine Empire persisted. The Fourth Crusade was redirected to Constantinople from its original goal of capturing Muslim-controlled Jerusalem by attacking Egypt. The Venetians, who played a crucial part in the Crusade by shipping the Crusaders, saw a chance to undercut their Byzantine rivals. Crusaders pillaged Constantinople in 1204 and expelled the Byzantines from the city for more than 50 years.

As a consequence, St. Mark's Basilica turned into a type of trophy case for Venice, housing the famed bronze horses and other stolen goods from the city of Constantinople.

Venice's Most Notable Traveler: Marco Polo
The renowned Venetian trader Marco Polo first appears in the narrative in the late 13th century. In 1269, Marco joined his father and uncle in their trade enterprise in Asia. After considerable travel in Asia, Marco eventually made his way back to Venice in 1295. He became the most well-known traveler in Venice because of his vast trip diaries, which gave Europeans a wealth of knowledge about other cultures, products, and technology.

The La Serenissima Glory Period (1297–1499 AD)

The Establishment of the Republic of Venice
A crucial turning point in the history of Venice occurred in the year 1297. In that year, the Venetian Republic came into being. This unusual

form of governance was not a democracy in the modern sense but rather a republic governed by an aristocracy. The aristocratic families had a solid grip on power despite the election of the Doge, or Duke. This type of administration emerged after a protracted development that was characterized by several changes intended to check the authority of the Doge and prevent the emergence of devoted family groups.

The Great Council, which had 45 members at first, progressively added additional delegates, and a convoluted election system was set up to choose the Doge. The Council of Ten, which was founded in 1310, functioned as a kind of internal police agency, maintaining aristocratic order and upholding the status quo. Despite its exclusivity, the Venetian Republic provided an example of how a republic might survive in the middle of a sea of monarchy for the Founding Fathers of the United States.

The Expansion of Venice: The Pinnacle of the Venetian Empire

During the Age of Exploration, the Venetian Republic's economic success encountered severe obstacles. Venetian territory was able to grow, nevertheless, across the Adriatic and into the eastern Mediterranean. Venetian influence and riches were able to grow as a result of this development, which put the city at odds with the mighty Ottoman Empire. The beginning of Venetian domination in the eastern Mediterranean may be traced to the Fourth Crusade, which destroyed Constantinople in 1204. Venice was expelled from Constantinople in 1261, but despite this, it continued to rule various Greek islands and ultimately regained some favor with Byzantium via a series of treaties.

'La Serenissima' and the Zenith of Venice

Venetian culture had achieved its pinnacle by the late 15th century. Venice, also known as "La Serenissima," or "The Most Serene," was a symbol of strength, prosperity, and culture. The spectacular architecture of the city, such as the Doge's Palace, which combines elements from all across the Mediterranean region, revealed the riches of the city. Famous Venetian painters like Tintoretto, whose works served as a reminder of the celestial benefits of excellent administration, decorated the palace's interior. At this period, Venice was more than simply a city; it was also a significant empire. The Venetian-Genoese war came to an end with the Peace of Turin in 1381, and Venice was left as the dominating force in the eastern Mediterranean, a position it would hold until the establishment of the Ottoman Empire.

Renaissance period in Venice (1500–1632 AD)

A Change in Venice's Fortunes Due to Ottoman Wars and Trade

In its heyday, trade and commerce were the lifeblood of Venice. However, Venice's fortunes underwent a huge change in the 16th century with the establishment of the Ottoman Empire. With their strategic grip over the Eastern Mediterranean, the Ottomans presented a serious threat to Venice's hegemony in commerce.

Venetian traders kept up strong business ties with the Ottomans despite the occasional wars, demonstrating the city's fortitude and flexibility. During this time of upheaval, the goal wasn't only to survive, but to thrive in the face of hardship.

Architectural Wonders: Venice's Glamour

The city's spectacular architecture was a reflection of the riches amassed over centuries of commerce. Venice was a magnificent and lovely city in the Renaissance. Beautiful palaces, elaborate cathedrals, and well-known structures like the Doge's Palace and St. Mark's Basilica dotted the cityscape. These magnificent buildings served as both a tribute to the city's artistic and cultural strength and as symbols of riches and power. Renowned architects like Mauro Codussi and Jacopo Sansovino rose to prominence during the Renaissance and left a lasting impression on the city. The San Zaccaria Church by Codussi and the St. Mark's Library by Sansovino are two outstanding examples of the Venetian Renaissance style, which is distinguished by balanced proportions and synthesis of Gothic and classical elements.

The Cultural Tapestry of Venice: Art and Politics

In Venice, the Renaissance was a time of intellectual and cultural flourishing. The city was a thriving center for philosophy, literature, and the arts. The aristocracy's dominance over Venice's political system had a big impact on the city's cultural scene. The Venetian Renaissance painters like Tintoretto and Titian decorated the halls of power with their masterpieces, demonstrating how often art was employed as a vehicle for political expression. The Doge's Palace was decorated with one of the biggest oil paintings in the world, Tintoretto's Paradise, while Titian's Assumption of the Virgin became the focal point of the Basilica di Santa Maria Gloriosa dei Frari. The way art and politics interacted gave Venice's cultural tapestry a fascinating new depth. As a result of the city's support for the arts, Venice became a center of culture throughout the Italian Renaissance, drawing thinkers and artists from all over Europe.

The Modern Era in Venice (1633–1700 AD)

An Era of Change: The Decline of Venice

The collapse of Venice began in the 17th century. The emergence of new powers in Europe posed a threat to the city's economic hegemony. New commercial routes had been created during the Age of Exploration, avoiding the Mediterranean and damaging Venice's strategic advantage.

Gondolas & Grand Tourists: The Appeal of Venice

Venice continued to be a city of charm and interest despite its dwindling authority. It became a well-liked vacation spot for affluent Europeans known as "Grand Tourists," who undertook protracted travels to see the continent's cultural gems, including the lavish and enigmatic Venetian Carnival. These tourists were attracted to the city because of its distinctive fusion of history, art, and culture. They were astounded by the city's architectural marvels, reveled in its energetic festivities, and gorged themselves on its delectable food. Gondolas, which have been a recognizable feature of Venice since the 11th century, have come to represent the city's elegance and are a favorite among visitors. Venice, despite being in decline, managed to retain its appeal and cultural relevance, demonstrating the city's tenacity and flexibility.

Venice's Resilience in the Face of Decline

Venice responded by making use of its cultural and historical resources in reaction to its waning influence. In addition to promoting itself as a destination for cultural tourism, the city made investments in the preservation of its architectural assets. By diversifying its economy, Venice also aimed to retain its economic viability. The city created businesses like glassmaking, lace blowing, and printing that benefited from its extensive creative heritage.

Venice's Turbulent Period (1700–1866)

Revolutionary Unrest: Venice's Independence War

For Venice, the 18th century was a time of great change. The stability of the city was disturbed by the French Revolutionary Wars, and the once-bustling Grand Tour routes became less active. The danger to the city went much beyond a simple decline in international tourists. A young French officer named Napoleon Bonaparte thought that the Venetian Republic had reached its breaking point in 1797. French soldiers pillaged the city and took numerous priceless works of art for their country. This was a turbulent time in Venice's history when the city was dealing with losing its freedom and having its cultural assets stolen.

When Did Venice Become a Part of Italy After Its Unification?

When the Venetian Republic was overthrown, Austrian control over Venice was established by 1815. However, Venice had a short proclamation of another republic when the 1840s revolutionary fever spread there. The Austrians suppressed this, but the rebellious spirit persisted. The Third Italian War of Freedom, which began in 1866, marked the culmination of the city's freedom effort. Otto von Bismarck, a politician from Prussia, assisted Venice in achieving independence from Austria and union with Italy. As a result, Venice had a tremendous period of change in its history, going from being a once-powerful republic to being a part of a single Italy.

A Living Museum of Venice Today (1866–Present)

Modernization in the Modern World: Venice
With the emergence of a new state came new rulers and plans for Venice's development. Famous Venetian businessmen like Count Giuseppe Volpi and Vittorio Cini brought electricity to Venice and created a variety of commercial possibilities, such as the renowned Venice Film Festival and a posh hotel chain. The

construction of the Santa Lucia Train Station, which connects Venice to the mainland, and the organization of one of Venice's most important events, the Venice Biennale, an international art exhibition that further solidified the city's cultural significance, were among the significant changes to the city's infrastructure.

Venice's Adaptation to Change: New Enterprises

Venice adapted and grew despite the difficulties of the 20th century, such as the Fascist rule and World War II. After the war, the city resumed hosting visitors from outside, retaining its reputation as a popular tourist destination. In addition, the city had to strike a balance between the necessity for growth and the need to preserve its historical and cultural assets.

Ancient Venice's Legacy: A Tour through Time

The rich heritage of Venice may be found all over the world. Venice has had a significant impact on global history, as seen by the US

Founding Fathers' use of it as inspiration while forming the fledgling US government and the legendary Venetian trader Marco Polo. The Lion of St. Mark and other Venice symbols may be seen throughout the Adriatic and the eastern Mediterranean, demonstrating the city's long-lasting influence on history. With its distinctive fusion of history, culture, and beauty, Venice continues to enthrall tourists today and serves as a living reminder of its illustrious past.

Reviewing Venice's History's Rich Tapestry
The narrative of Venice's history is a compelling one of tenacity, inventiveness, and adaptation. The city expanded from its little beginnings in the Venetian lagoon to become a significant force in the Mediterranean, with influence far-reaching beyond its swampy roots. The Grand Canal functioned as the city's principal thoroughfare, teeming with trade and commerce and a tribute to Venetian engineering and prosperity.

Venice became a key trade hub because of its advantageous position and skilled diplomacy. Venetian traders built up extensive networks for trading items from the East and the West. The city's expansion and ability to forge a distinctive character in a world that was changing quickly were both fueled by the enormous riches this commerce brought to the area. Like all great powers, Venice faded, however. The Venetian economy was weakened by the discovery of new trade routes across Africa and the development of new powers in Europe. Despite these obstacles, Venice showed a remarkable capacity for adaptation. The city managed to reinvent itself while in decline, keeping its attraction and charm.

Even while Venetian wealth isn't as readily apparent in the nation's economy now, it is evident in the city's extensive cultural history, stunning architecture, and long-lasting influence. Venice, a city carved out of the water and shaped by the tides of history, stands as a tribute to the tenacious spirit of La Serenissima and never ceases to captivate and inspire.

Inspiring the Spirit of Adventure: Why Visit Venice

Venice is more than just a city; it is a vibrant illustration of human ingenuity and the allure of history. Whether you're a history buff, an architect, or simply searching for a unique holiday, Venice offers a wide range of choices for inquiry and exploration. From the richness of St. Mark's Square to the tranquil appeal of its lesser-known rivers, Venice exhorts you to let yourself be swept away by its ageless beauty.

We hope that your desire for adventure has been whetted by this historical tour of Venice. If you are driven to discover more about the city's interesting past and dynamic present, why not start making vacation plans right away? And never forget that immersing yourself in the city's history and letting it come to life all around you is the best way to experience Venice.

Location of Venice

Travelers have been enthralled by Venice for ages because it is an extraordinary and captivating location. Italy's northeastern region contains this city. The city is renowned for its complex system of canals. Venice's character and allure are significantly shaped by its terrain.

Where and How It Is Forme: Within the Venetian Lagoon is where Venice is located. This enclosed bay on the Adriatic Sea is located in the Veneto region of Italy. Six historical administrative districts make up Venice's historic center. These are referred to as "sestieri" (plural: "sestiere"). There are 118 little islands in the city. These islands are connected by a sophisticated system of canals and bridges. Sestieri owns several of these islands. For instance, Dorsoduro is the owner of the island of Giudecca. Once again, San Giorgio Maggiore, the cemetery island, is part of the San Marco sestiere. Additionally, some islands are divided into sestieri, like Burano, which has five. One may classify the Sestiere as an Italian neighborhood. The lagoon is shielded by the Lido, a lengthy barrier island. The Lido serves as a natural barrier between the city and the ocean, protecting it from storm surges.

Waterways & Canals: Remember that navigating Venice is challenging and requires some adjustment time. In Venice, only water buses and water taxis are available. Venice's canals are the heart and soul of the city. These are acting as its main mode of transportation. The biggest and most significant canal is the Grand Canal. It divides the city in half as it meanders across the center of the city. The city is crisscrossed by several smaller canals that confusingly link different islands and neighborhoods. Over 400 bridges cross the city's canals, adding to the beautiful attractiveness of the area.

Problems of Living on the Water: Venice is hardly the only place where living near water presents difficulties. The city is vulnerable to acqua alta, or high tides, which may cause flooding in low-lying regions. Raised wooden walkways, or "catwalks," are used in similar situations to aid locals and guests in navigating the flooded streets. Venetian engineers have used a variety of strategies throughout the years to mitigate the effects of increasing water levels.

The city's ancient structures and infrastructure are also in danger due to the frequent exposure to water and dampness. To prevent the deterioration of these priceless sites, maintenance and repair work are underway.

Without a doubt, Venice's topography plays a crucial role in how it is known as the "Floating City." Its canals, stunning bridges, and old buildings provide tourists with an amazing experience. The city continues to amaze the globe with its timeless beauty and rich cultural legacy, despite the particular difficulties brought on by its placement on the sea.

What are Venice's top three fascinating facts?

Venice has a lot of interesting facts. To begin with, it is completely built on a lagoon with 118 islands. The old city of Venice was built carefully on an island.

Second, there are no roads for cars in Venice. Boats are the main mode of transportation on these waterways. This distinguishes it as one of the unique transportation systems in the world.

The annual Carnival of Venice is another notable event held in the city. One of them is the Carnival of Venice, where vibrant costumes and exquisite masks create a fantasy atmosphere that attracts tourists from across the world. These intriguing characteristics contribute to Venice's enduring charm.

Why is Venice arranged that way?
Venice is a fantastic historical site from the Middle Ages. In the Middle Ages, the city was constructed on top of a lagoon to give defense against invading armies. The dikes in the lagoon provided defense against enemy ottomans for the

Venetians. This sea is naturally protected by the islands. Venice saw several geographic changes throughout time. The city's canals were used as a conduit for travel. The boat is the primary vehicle. The inventiveness of Venice's founders is still evident in the unique design of the city today, which has contributed much to its ongoing appeal and attractiveness.

CHAPTER 2

Getting ready and making plans for your trip

Ways to go to Venice

As one of Italy's most visited cities, there are several methods to reach the City of Canals, including by car, rail, bus, and airline. Despite being a tiny island, Venice has excellent connections to both the mainland and the rest of the globe because of its significant tourist sector. The simplest routes to take to reach Venice are as follows:

By aircraft

One of the busiest airfields in Italy is Marco Polo International Airport, which serves Venice. The "Queen of the Adriatic" may also be reached via the Treviso Airport, which is about an hour's drive north of Venice.

Traveling from the United States: Several airlines provide direct flights from the United States to Venice's Marco Polo Airport, however, the majority of them only operate in the peak seasons (spring, summer, and fall), such as Delta Airlines and US Airways:

- Delta Airlines offers nonstop service from New York's JFK Airport.
- US Airways offers nonstop service out of Philadelphia.
- Offering connecting flights from New York, Boston, and Miami is Alitalia.

If you're coming from Canada, Air Canada and other airlines like Lufthansa link several Canadian cities with Venice with nonstop flights between Toronto and Venice (Marco Polo Airport). The most common departure cities are Montreal (typically 2 stops, 14 hours), Toronto (typically 2 stops, 17 hours), and Vancouver.

No airlines provide direct flights from Australia to Venice or Italy. However, a few of businesses provide flights with just one stop:

- **Adelaide:** Flights with one or two stops are available from Emirates and Etihad Airways; the trip takes around 24 hours.
- **Brisbane:** Flights with up to three stops are available from Emirates and Etihad Airways; the trip takes roughly 30 hours.
- **Melbourne:** Flights with two or three stops are available from Qatar Airways, Emirates, and KLM (travel time: 30 hours).
- **Perth:** Flights with one or two stops are available from Emirates, Qatar Airways, Air France, and KLM (travel time is around 25 hours).
- **Sydney:** Flights with one to three stops are available from Alitalia, Emirates, KLM, and Air France (around 30 hours total).

Traveling from Europe: If you reside in the United Kingdom, several airlines provide direct flights to Venice from several places around the nation. The flight from southern England takes around two hours. The major low-cost carriers serving Venice are:

- From Bristol, East Midlands, Leeds Bradford, and London Stansted, Ryanair provides direct flights.
- From Bristol, Edinburgh, London Gatwick, London Luton, and Manchester, EasyJet provides direct flights.
- British Airways links Venice Marco Polo Airport with London Heathrow, London Gatwick, and London City.

Find out how to travel to the city center from Marco Polo Airport or Treviso Airport after you have booked your trip and know which airport you will arrive at:

1. The Venice Marco Polo Airport is situated eight kilometers (4.3 miles) to the north of Venice. The busiest international airport in Venice is there.

2. Low-cost airlines like Ryanair and Wizz Air often fly out of the Treviso Airport,

which is 25 miles (40 km) north of Venice.

By train

The "Serenissima" may also be reached by rail. Venice's main train station, Venezia Santa Lucia, links the city with many other nations and Italian cities. It's an intriguing choice since you can fly cheaply to Milan and then take the train from there to Venice. The train is also the fastest and most relaxing method to reach Rome or Florence, making it a fantastic choice for those who want to see the nation.

Railway Station in Venezia Santa Lucia: Venezia Venice's primary rail station is Santa Lucia Railway Station. Venice is connected to several important Italian cities via the train station. On the official TGV or Ferrovie dello Stato websites, you may see train timetables, and rates, and purchase tickets online:
- Ferrovie dello Stato
- TGV Europe

By Vehicle

Given that just a portion of the island can be reached by car, Venice isn't the greatest spot to drive to. You must thus park your vehicle in one of the following lots:

- Garage San Marco, located in Piazzale Roma, costs €30 (£26) per day.
- Parking garage Autorimessa Comunale at Piazzale Roma, costing €23.40 (£20.30) per day.
- On the island of Tronchetto, there is a garage. You may save money by getting the Rolling Venice Card. Each day, it costs € 21 (£ 18.20).

Before crossing the Ponte della Libertà, there are less expensive parking spots (in the industrial park, to the right) that cost less than €10 (£8.70) per day. The locals and Italians like this choice the most. From these parking areas, you may buy a bus ticket to the city center. You must take a vaporetto from Piazzale Roma, where all the buses are available, to go to your accommodation.

Venice Travel Requirements

If you want to know when, in the opinion of a local, is the ideal time to visit Venice based on the weather, events that are taking place, and the cost of transport and lodging.

What time of year is ideal for visiting Venice?
The first response would be that spring and the beginning of October are the ideal times to visit Venice. Even in the winter or during times of high tide (often referred to as "acqua alta"), the city is always worth visiting.

I suggest going to Venice from the end of March to the beginning of June, as well as from September to the middle of October. The temperature ranges between 15 and 25 °C, which is ideal for strolling around the city, seeing sites, and organizing a few day excursions. The summer months are best avoided since while the temperature may easily get beyond 27 °C, the excessive humidity makes it seem much warmer than it is.

In actuality, Venice has a somewhat continental climate, with hot and steamy summers and chilly, damp winters. The Adriatic Sea helps to moderate the heat but keep in mind that Venice is located inside of a lagoon, therefore the city is always humid.

The ideal times to visit Venice if money is your primary concern are March and April in the spring and October and November in the fall. High tides might occur in the fall, which discourages many travelers from going at this time of year.

Venetian currency

Your trip to Venice is powered by money, so it's a good idea to be familiar with some fundamental guidelines about cash, currency exchange, and credit cards before you go.

Cash: Italy is a member of the Euro zone. Use the local money instead of being one of the idiots who try to pay Italians with dollars or pounds sterling, exactly as you would expect foreign tourists to do at home.

Cashpoint: The best place to get cash is at a "bancomat," which is Italian for "automated teller machine" (ATM) or "cashpoint." All across the city, ATMs are located on bank structures, and the majority of them offer multilingual instructions.

Here are some pointers for utilizing ATMs:
Verify that your home bank is aware of your travels. If they aren't informed in advance, some banks purportedly prohibit overseas transactions for security concerns. Bancomats with the logos of Cirrus, Plus, Maestro, and other global ATM networks should be sought out. Only account holders may withdraw cash from machines at the Cassa di Risparmio di Venezia, a local savings organization with several branches.

Be ready to enter a PIN with a four-digit numeric. Ask your bank to update your PIN or provide you with guidelines for using ATMs abroad if your bank demands a six-digit PIN or utilizes a mix of letters and numbers. Users of international cards may be required to choose "International card" on certain bancomat menus before withdrawing money. (This is okay--you're only verifying that the machine has to connect with an international ATM network).

Be advised that many banks charge several percent in surcharges and transaction fees for cash withdrawals made outside of their networks. Change banks if your current one is greedy. Carry ATM cards from two different banks, if you can, in case one of your cards isn't accepted. (Also, grab additional cash before you're about to become bankrupt; occasionally, foreign ATM networks are out for a few hours.)

The greatest exchange rates are almost usually found at ATMs or cash machines when exchanging cash for local currency. Hotel front desks and currency exchange bureaus sometimes provide inadequate rates and exorbitant charges. The Travelex office in Venice was charging an 8.5 percent commission on U.S. dollar notes plus a handling charge of €3.50 last time we looked. Try to restrict the amount of cash or traveler's checks you exchange if you must, since doing so twice (from your currency to euros and back again) will result in two significant commission fees.

Using credit cards: The majority of stores and eateries accept Visa and MasterCard; however, smaller businesses, certain local eateries or pubs, and food sellers may not. (Also, gratuities at restaurants are often made in cash.) Higher-end shops and eateries that serve visitors accept American Express.

Warnings:
Foreign transaction fees are now typically charged by the majority of credit card providers and may be as high as 4%. Use the credit card with the lowest fee, if you have several credit

cards, for your travel. (We often use Capital One, which doesn't charge American cardholders a premium.)

Some credit card companies won't authorize overseas transactions unless you've informed them in advance of your trip. Before leaving, it's a good idea to phone the toll-free number on the back of your card to double-check that it will be accepted overseas.

Keeping your things safe

Although muggings and robberies are rare in Venice, pickpockets, purse snatchers, and camera thieves are widespread, particularly in popular tourist sites like the Piazza San Marco and the train station. Avoid being overt about pulling out your money in public by keeping the majority of it concealed under your shirt in a "neck safe" together with your passport, credit cards, and ATM cards.

CHAPTER 3

In 2024, some advice for a fantastic trip to Venice, Italy

Important Travel Advice For A Fantastic Trip

Are you traveling to Venice and unsure about how to get there from the airport, how to save money, or what to bring? You're at the proper location! I've made many trips to the Floating City, so I've collected some invaluable travel advice that will help you make the most of your vacation.

What to Bring: A widespread myth holds that Venice is always busy. Although there are usually more people in the city during the summer, you may escape them by going to Venice in the spring or autumn. In such a case, be ready for colder weather. The following are some necessities to bring:

- **Bring nice clothing**

Venice is undoubtedly one of the world's most fashionable cities, so you'll want to look the part. Bring a couple of classy clothes with you. Having said that, don't forget to consider your comfort. Bring some shoes so you may easily wander about.

- **Pack an umbrella for travel**

Whatever time of year you go, don't forget to bring your travel umbrella! You don't want to be caught unprepared in the rain. You may pick between taking a bus, cab, or boat from the Venice Marco Polo Airport to the city center or Mestre (a village on the mainland that faces Venice and is likely where you will be staying).

- **Water Transportation Is An Option To Get To Venice**

You may take a public boat from the airport to Venice since the city's principal streets are canals. You should budget around €15 per person one way and €17 roundtrip. Given that the boat may stop many times along the journey, this is quite realistic but can take some time.

- **Taking the Bus Saves Money**

The bus from the airport is a more affordable option. You may expect to pay between €8 and €15 for the roundtrip. Typically, the bus ride from the airport to Venice takes 20 minutes.

- **If you are carrying a lot of luggage, taxis are your best option**

Regular taxis are also available from the airport to Venice, with Piazzale Roma as their last destination (this is the terminal where all motorized vehicles arrive or depart from Venice). You'll pay between €35 to €40 for a cab. If you're taking large amounts of baggage, this is the best choice.

How to Get Around in Venice: Venice is the largest pedestrian city in the world, but how can one get around in a place where there are reputedly more boats than cars? Here are the steps to take.

- **Walking Is The Best Way To See Venice**

On foot is the greatest method to see everything that Venice has to offer as a historical city. Many Venetians are active and healthy because they walk about a lot, even though this may seem like a health pitch. You'll be able to thoroughly explore the city by walking as well. You'll pass by lovely tiny bridges and canals that you would otherwise miss if traveling by gondola or water bus along the route. In other words, exploring this beautiful city on foot will offer you the chance to stumble across some of the hidden jewels.

- **Use the Vaporetto (water bus) to go about**

This is the second-best and, sometimes, the sole method of transportation. With a single ticket (valid for 75 minutes) costing around €7.50, a Vaporetto will suit you well whether you want to travel to Murano, Burano, or Lido. These tickets may be purchased at the ticket booths outside the Rialto rail station or the vending machines in front of the major stops. Additionally, you may get them from newsstands and tobacco stores.

- **Rather than using public transportation, take a ride on a gondola or a sandolo**

Traditional Venetian boats called gondola and sandolo may be used to visit the city from its well-known canals. There are several options for rides, which typically last 30 minutes and cost approximately €80 per boat. Gondolas, on the other hand, are just used for elegant trips and are not always utilized to get somewhere, unlike water buses or taxis. They'll give you a chance to see the city's picturesque neighborhoods and small canals before returning to their boarding station rather than transporting you anywhere. Six passengers can fit inside a gondola, including the gondolier. To save some money, don't forget to haggle for the gondola or ride with other visitors.

Language Hints: Compared to a city like Rome, Venice has fewer residents who can speak

English well. That could be a result of their constant juggling between Venetian and Italian languages.

Fortunately, people who work in the tourism sector can converse with visitors in adequate English. However, learning a few words and phrases in Venetian may greatly enhance your experience.

- **Practice a Few Italian Words and Phrases**

Are you an English speaker? – Te parli inglexe?

Speak any Venetian? – Párlitu venetian?

What does this cost? – Cuanto Cóstelo?

Kindly – Per Piasser

I'm sorry – El me Scuxa

Thank you – Grazie

Enjoy your travels – Bon viaxo!

I have no idea – No só

Enjoy your food – Bon apetito!

Goodbye – Adio

Tipping in Venice: If you're visiting Venice, tipping can be one of your top worries. In general, Italians don't leave a lot of money at the end of the meal, thus leaving too little might be seen as impolite while leaving too much could be seen as haughty.

- **A Heartfelt Tip**

For this reason, as a genuine act of gratitude, we advise tipping from the heart. Therefore, it would be excellent to provide anything between €5 and €10 when the service is outstanding. There is so much to see and do in Venice that you'll never get bored!

- **Eat Like A Venetian**

The fact that visitors outnumber Venetians year-round is no longer a secret. 20 million visitors visit Venice annually, compared to 60,000 locals. However, dining out and trying genuine Venetian cuisines is worthwhile if you still want to eat like a Venetian. Of course, doing a culinary tour is the simplest way to learn how to eat like a Venetian. It's a good chance to sample local food, explore the area, and connect with other adventurers.

Pro tip: Visit a Bacaro or Osteria for a genuine dining experience. These are little bars where you may have a glass of wine and food for less money. Also, bear in mind that sit-down restaurants are pricey; instead, order at the counter as most Italians and Venetians do to pay less.

- **Travel to Riva Degli Schiavoni, Bridge Of Sighs, and Piazza San Marco**

The most popular tourist destinations in Venice are often packed, as you've certainly heard several times. These locations are historically significant and unforgettable, and I strongly advise you not to skip them because so many people never have the chance to see them. Starting before dawn will ensure that you have these locations to yourself. Alternatively, get skip-the-line tickets and a guided tour to avoid the throng.

- **Wander Around Alone**

We assure you that even seasoned visitors sometimes get disoriented in Venice. Be at ease about being lost, however. You never know what you could discover by mistake if you explore the city! Overall, the secret to having fun in Venice is to have an open mind, be prepared to get lost in the winding alleyways and understand that canals serve as the city's primary thoroughfare. You are, after all, in Venice!

Things Tourists Should Never Do in Venice: Venice receives a large number of visitors each year, and there is sometimes some cultural tension between visitors and residents. It's understandable why some travelers grumble about being taken advantage of by con artists. Here is a short list of things not to do in Venice that will help you move about the city with elegance.

- **Take a canal swim**

The water may appear tempting, but this is a demonstrably awful decision. The canals are public roadways, thus you might suffer catastrophic injuries from a passing boat's propeller. Second, due to Venice's antiquated sewage infrastructure, all garbage from residences and accommodations is dumped into the lagoon. Not to mention that it is unlawful, which means you risk receiving a large fine.

- **Travel to August**

The neighborhood eateries, stores, and bars will all be closed for Ferraogosto in August due to extreme humidity. During this period, everyone who lives here departs, leaving the city a deserted playground for the hordes of visitors who will swarm the area. Venezia is far more beautiful in the spring, autumn, or winter, so visit then to see it.

- **Inquire as to when Venice shuts**

This question has probably been posed to every Venetian who works in the tourist industry, and it may be the ultimate ignorant emblem. They want to yell back," People live then!" Irrespective of how beautiful it is, people who approach Venice as a living, breathing megacity will have a far better experience.

- **Plan on paying with a card**

Even if they do, cash is always recommended since some of this city's top pubs, stores, and restaurants don't take credit cards. This also reflects the reality that small, family-run companies are still very much a part of American society. Carry cash if you want to participate, and don't be shocked if someone asks for spare change.

- **Touch the vegetation**

To gain a better perspective of the canal, you may be enticed to descend a few of the stairs along the water's edge. The green substance on the stones is seaweed, and it may be misleadingly slippery. You don't want to be one of the several tourists who fell into the canal while attempting to take a picture.

- **Take a seat on a bridge or in an alley**

Venice has a small-town infrastructure while being a global metropolis, which may cause issues with traffic flow. Walking is the primary mode of transportation in this area. Therefore, sitting down on a bridge or in a small alley is the same as halting your automobile on a four-lane highway. Sit in the campi, where there are more public spaces available. Make sure you are aware of the area that you or your group are occupying and whether or not you are impeding traffic, whether you are in a store or an alley. When traveling through tight streets, the basic guideline is to keep to the right. This city has little space, therefore it's wise to exercise additional consideration.

- **Purchase shoddy products**

People will never stop attempting to pass off mass-produced goods as the genuine thing in Venice. You'll find American machine-made masks, Chinese "Murano" glass, and factory-style oil paintings created by low-paid laborers. Something may be a fraud if it is unexpectedly inexpensive. Use your common sense and do thorough research to avoid falling into one of these tourist traps. Along with receiving something of genuine worth, you'll also be helping individuals who are working honestly and virtuously.

- **Consume meals where visitors are present**

A restaurant will be pricey and not great if none of the patrons are locals. Regardless of whether you like to plan or are more spontaneous, use your best judgment when deciding where to eat. You can tell whether a pub or restaurant is going to be excellent by how busy it is with locals.

- **Dump rubbish on the sidewalk**

Although it seems quite obvious, you'd be surprised at how much trash is dumped on the street in utterly unsuitable locations. At the end of the day, windowsills will have empty bottles, napkins, and ice cream cups lined them or resting on top of wells. Just hang onto your rubbish until you can properly dispose of it; public trash cans are easy to find throughout the city and are often found in the larger campi and along key roadways. Consider how much waste you are producing as well, particularly about plastic bottles. You don't need to purchase water in bottles since the public fountains contain drinking water, which is a useful suggestion.

- **Continue along the beaten route**

Numerous marked pathways are mostly for visitors in Venice, but many undiscovered streets are teeming with local activity. You must be ready to get lost, to go down obscure side streets not seen on maps, and to wander if you want to see a real, lived-in city.

- **Eat pizza**

Since wood-burning ovens have traditionally been prohibited in Venice for fire safety concerns, it may be extremely difficult to obtain decent pizza there. The majority of pizza restaurants are tourist traps unless it's one of the few locations that does it well. That serves as a further reminder that Venice had independence for most of its history and that its cuisine deviates from the typical perceptions of Italian cuisine.

- **Get a cup of coffee to go**

In Italy, there is simply no justification for drinking coffee in a take-out cup. An espresso may be consumed in a matter of seconds, whereas a cappuccino can be savored slowly over two minutes. What's the rush, too? You may take some time to unwind and drink your coffee in a real cup if you have the time to go get one.

- **Maintain your comfort level**

Put yourself to the test! You might spend the whole of your trip here in a tourist bubble, taking in only hazy impressions of everyday life in Venice. However, Venice is there in front of you, so what's the point? This city is unusual and odd for all the bizarre and unusual reasons that it is. This has no guide, just like it's impossible to chart Venice's back streets. A keen and open mind must actively seek out this city's greatest features.

CHAPTER 4

Getting around Venice

The Easy Guide to Getting Around Venice, Italy

Navigating a city without vehicles, like Venice. The largest pedestrian city in the world is Venice. In terms of sustainable transportation, Venice is at the top in Italy. More people use public transportation than private transportation here than anyplace else in Italy.

What are the finest methods for getting about Venice on your next trip? Learn more below.

- **Getting around on foot in Venice**

Walking is the most convenient method to get to Venice, Italy. In reality, getting to Venice on foot is nearly always the fastest option. Although it may seem like a health promotion, Venetians are typically healthy and active since they go almost exclusively on foot. It's a rare chance to see

Venice's little bridges, canals, and secret attractions that a water bus would normally pass by.

- **The "vaporetto," a waterbus, is used to get about Venice.**

By water, the bus is the second-best way to get to Venice. Every day of the year, public service is available. Every ten minutes throughout the day, water bus stations on Venice's Grand Canal are serviced. Every 20 minutes, service is provided to the islands of Lido, Murano, and Burano. Water bus stations are visited every 20 and 40 minutes at night.

The cost of a water bus ride in Venice

An individual ticket for the Venice city water bus line costs 7.50€. Since you validated the ticket at the ticket machine, it is now valid for 75 minutes. Once authorized, you get 75 minutes to ride the waterbus as many times as you want.

There are various locations in Venice where you may purchase water bus tickets:

- at the stalls with sellers outside of all the major water bus stations.
- at ticket booths located outside the Rialto Bridge, Saint Mark's, and the Venice train station. Use these offices to buy your tickets and ask any queries you may have.
- over the city, in tobacco stores and newspaper kiosks.

Day tickets for the Venice water bus are also available:
- The cost of the one-day ticket is 20 euros, and it is good for 24 hours.
- The 48-hour, 30€ 2-day pass is valid for both days.
- Three days span 72 hours and cost 40 euros.
- The 60€ seven-day pass is valid for seven days.

Unfortunately, there are often large lines at ticket offices and vending machines. If you are unable to buy a ticket there, you may do it while riding the water bus!

In such a situation, be careful: As soon as you board the water bus, tell the sailor that you must purchase tickets. If you don't, you risk receiving a large fine! Since there is no other option to pay aboard, bring cash.

- **Using a water taxi to get to Venice**

Because of their very high fixed costs, locals in Venice avoid using taxis. Tourists who prefer the convenience of private transportation versus using public waterbus nearly exclusively hire taxis. Typically, a taxi journey costs between 100 and 130 euros for up to 4 passengers. Taxis may hold up to 10 people, however, after the fifth passenger, there is an additional price. Each passenger pays around 15 euros.

In conclusion, taxis are more comfortable and intimate than waterbuses but cost more money. The cost of the water bus from the airport is 15 euros per person, thus a party of 8 to 10 individuals traveling to Venice might think about using a water taxi. As a result, the cost for a larger party to get to Venice by taxi or water bus is not much different, but a water taxi will stop directly at their destination.

- **Gondola and sandolo travel in Venice**

In Venice, "sandoli" and gondolas are not considered modes of transportation. Instead, these are exclusive boat cruises for sightseeing. Numerous spots across the city provide sandolo and gondola trips. Rides run 30 minutes, cost 80 euros per boat, and provide stunning views of the region.

With the gondoliere or "sandolista" at the wheel, a gondola or sandolo may accommodate up to 6 people. Unlike a water bus or a taxi, a gondola is not utilized for transportation; instead, it returns to its boarding point. The most well-known historic Venetian craft are gondolas, which formerly served as the equivalent of horse-drawn carriages in other towns. Similar to gondola excursions, "sandolo" trips take place on a distinct kind of Venetian boat called a "sandolo."

The "gondola da traghetto" is the only gondola trip that is not included. A "traghetto" is a gondola fare service that allows you to go across Venice's Grand Canal. Three sites still provide a "traghetto" service as of right now.

Where to Sleep in Venice

A guide to the neighborhood and area of Venice, Italy

In Venice, there are a ton of fantastic lodging options, many of which are close to the city's top attractions. The stunning Venetian Gothic architecture may be seen whether you explore the streets, cross the Rialto Bridge, or take a memorable gondola ride. You may add a ton of breathtaking places to your agenda for Venice.

However, you must choose a location to stay in before boarding an aircraft and traveling to

Venice. Each of Venice's many neighborhoods has its beauty and is located at varying distances from various attractions. You'll find a list of Venice's neighborhoods and the top hotels nearby in this guide. Here is a brief list of Venice's neighborhoods. For a more thorough explanation of hotels and Airbnb and the kind of tourists they're best suited for, continue reading below.

San Marco is the best destination for first-timers. You'll be in the heart of the city with easy access to most major attractions.

Santa Croce: An ideal position near incoming, outgoing, and local transit.

Castello is the ideal destination for tourists seeking peace and charm in a small town.

San Polo – Located near most attractions and in the city center as well. This neighborhood is home to the Rialto Market and Bridge.

Best for budget-conscious vacationers is Cannaregio. Venice's Jewish ghetto and Santa Lucia rail station are both located here.

The city's main attractions are only a short stroll over the Grand Canal from Dorsoduro, which is home to many outstanding galleries and museums.

Great for beach lovers is Lido. Lido is a fantastic spot to vacation in the summer since it boasts beautiful beaches that extend for kilometers.

Giudecca – A more tranquil neighborhood with a laid-back nightlife. Excellent if you prefer a slower pace yet still want to visit the major sights via Vaporetto or water bus.

- **San Marco**

One of the nicest locations to stay in Venice is unquestionably San Marco, particularly for first-time tourists. It is a booming tourist hub in the center of Venice and is close to all the main tourist attractions. There are usually too many people in this area. San Marco is the ideal location to appreciate the commotion of people around you.

This region is home to a variety of unusual attractions. Here is where Saint Mark's Basilica is located, and it serves as a superb illustration of Byzantine architecture. It exhibits the enormous riches and power of former Venetian monarchs and links to Palazzo Ducale, also known as the Doge's Palace.

Take a trip under the renowned clock tower at Saint Mark's, Torre dell'Orologio. After that, you may stop by the 18th-century-founded Caffé Florian for a cup of coffee. Make sure to take your time, since the price of your coffee includes the cost of the "atmosphere".

Depending on where you stay, the hotels in San Marco may vary from budget to luxury. The cost of lodging increases with proximity to Saint Mark's. Therefore, if you wish to stay in San Marco while visiting Venice, preparation and saving are crucial. Watch for savings and off-season hotel specials. "Best suited for first-time guests".

Lodging around San Marco

Luxurious: The St. Regis Venice, a 5-star hotel with stunning Grand Canal views.

Mid-range: Approximately 150 feet separate the Hotel Montecarlo, a 3-star hotel with Venetian-style rooms, from Piazza San Marco (Saint Mark's Square).

Budget-friendly: Hotel ai do Mori Venice, a charming 1-star hotel located 350 feet from Saint Mark's Square.

- **Santa Croce**

A little area of Venice called Santa Croce is conveniently located near the city's transit center. It has maintained its unique charm, which is evident in the neighborhood's architecture. Staying in this area is quite handy, particularly if you want to see additional places of interest throughout your vacation. In addition to the Santa Lucia rail station and the bus station at Piazzale Roma in Santa Croce, it is simple to cross the Ponte degli Scalzi to board a train.

To begin with, Santa Croce itself has a lot of attractions. Don't forget to see the eerie, enigmatic San Giacomo dell'Orio church from the ninth century. The fact that this church has undergone several rebuildings throughout the ages has given rise to its distinctive architectural styles. Additionally, there is the Palazzo Mocenigo, a palace constructed for the Mocenigo dynasty, Doges of Venice.

Museum enthusiasts, don't give up. You may tour several museums in this region. From the Natural History Museum to Ca' Pesaro, home of the International Galleria of Modern Art and the Museo d'Arte Orientale.

Additionally, Santa Croce offers some of the greatest seafood meals. You won't get hungry in this area since there are so many delicious native Venetian restaurants. A well-liked restaurant with outdoor dining that looks out over a pretty little canal is Osteria Ae Saracche. The cost of lodging is reasonable. There are various wonderful cheap, mid-priced, and luxurious hotels in the region. If hotels are not your thing, there are also condos and Airbnb's. "Best for: Vacationers who wish to see more of Venice".

Lodging in Santa Croce

Luxury: Hotel Canal Grande, a 4-star boutique hotel that once served as a palace.

Mid-Range: Hotel Aquarius Venice, a 4-star establishment with a stunning garden in the heart of Venice.

Budget: Hotel Locanda Salieri, a charming little place with stunning views and nice accommodations.

- **Castello**

The biggest neighborhood in Venice is called Castello. The region runs from Venice's eastern edge to the western city center. The location is also the quietest and is regarded as being off the main path. There is plenty of room to move about, and fewer visitors are impeding your progress. Castello offers a wealth of breathtaking sites for visitors to enjoy.

The largest street in Venice, Via Garibaldi, is accessible by foot. As the sun sets, a magnificent evening scene also emerges on this street. In Castello, you may also explore a lot of tiny boutiques and artisan stores. Additionally, one of the outdoor markets is a great place to pick up a tasty Venetian treat for a snack.

The Museo Storico Navale will appeal to history aficionados. This museum has a sizable collection of antique ships, commercial objects, and gondolas. Anyone who appreciates boats and maritime history will love it. The Arsenale di Venezia, which houses the shipbuilding industry of Venice, is located in Castello.

Unfortunately, it is only accessible to the public during the Biennale art display and is presently being utilized by the Italian army.

Speaking of the Biennale, these yearly displays of art and architecture are held in Castello's gardens. Biennale may imply "held every two years," yet this yearly international event is hosted in Venice. The display is the kind that alternates between art and architecture on the odd and even years, respectively, every two years. Festivals for music, dance, theater, and cinema are among the other well-liked events.

Due to the wide selection of low-cost and mid-range hotels in Castello, lodging may be reasonably inexpensive. AirBnBs and apartments are also available nearby. There are magnificent luxury hotels accessible for you to stay in if you want something more opulent. "Best for Vacationers looking for a relaxing vacation in a serene area".

Lodging around Castello

Luxury: Only a 6-minute walk separates the 4-star Hotel Ai Cavalieri di Venezia from Saint Mark's Square in the heart of Venice.

Mid-Range: Hotel Da Bruno, a charming little 3-star establishment located midway between Saint Mark's Square and the Rialto Bridge.

Cost-effective: Hotel Rio, a lovely boutique hotel in the center of Venice.

- **San Polo**

San Polo is the smallest neighborhood in Venice. But it doesn't imply there isn't anything to do or see in this place. You can quickly go to Dorsoduro, Santa Croce, and the Grand Canal since these sites are bordered by the neighborhood. Despite being modest, it is in a great position in the heart of Venice. It features wonderful churches, restaurants, shops, and museums, and is near to all the major attractions. The Rialto Market, a fruit, vegetable, and seafood market in San Polo, is extremely well-known. In restaurants and pubs around the market, you may enjoy some delectable Venetian cuisine and pair it with a drink of Prosecco.

San Polo is the home of the fabled Rialto Bridge. Since it was initially built in 1591, this bridge, which is located in Venice, has seen the greatest traffic. The Rialto Bridge's spectacular architecture is in the traditional Renaissance style. According to several historians, San Giacomo di Rialto Church in San Polo is Venice's oldest continuously operational church. But it's still unknown how old this church is.

There are several fantastic low-cost and mid-range hotel alternatives in this neighborhood. AirBnBs and inexpensive flats are also available nearby. The Vaporetto, a water taxi that is a popular mode of transit in Venice, is accessible from this area. "Best for Vacationers seeking a more tranquil setting near the major attractions".

Lodging in San Polo

Luxury: Four-star H10 Palazzo Canova is a luxurious hotel on the Grand Canal that is close to Rialto Bridge.

Mid-Range: Hotel Marconi, a charming boutique hotel just across the Rialto Bridge with a stunning view.

Budget-friendly: Riva del Vin Boutique Hotel - Cute tiny hotel with nice staff.

- **Cannaregio**

A portion of Venice known for its popularity is Cannaregio. It can be because of the neighborhood's affordable housing options or its proximity to the major train station. This may make transportation and travel extremely easy, but the surroundings may become less appealing as you approach the station.

However, Cannaregio's attraction extends beyond its cost and accessibility to transit. This area is always bustling with residents and tourists. Any visitor to Venice will find Cannaregio to have a lot to offer, from delectable dining choices to breathtaking scenery.

Start by trying some authentic Venetian friton. Most vendors in Cannaregio provide this specialty, which is simply fried fish in a paper cone. then go for a shopping spree on the Strada Nuova. When visiting Venice, be sure to go along Calle Varisco. It is located in Strada Nuova and is Venice's tiniest street.

Alternatively, you might go to Fondamenta Ormesini. Here, you may unwind and enjoy some delicious Venetian cuisine while people-watching. Alternatively, if you'd like, you may take a leisurely walk here. The Jewish Quarter, often known as the Venetian Ghetto, continues to be the area's most visited destination. Jews were forcefully separated and sent to this little region of Venice in the sixteenth century. Shakespeare's play The Merchant of Venice is credited with popularizing it.

As previously indicated, lodging in this location is rather inexpensive. For vacationers on a tight budget, it is ideal. There are several attractions to view, and getting to Venice is easy with the help of the public transit system. Here, it's simple to find cheap lodging options including hotels, apartments, and Airbnb. "Best for: Budget-conscious tourists".

Lodging in Cannaregio

Luxury: In the Jewish ghetto, there is a sophisticated 4-star hotel called Carnival Palace.

Mid-Range: The 4-star boutique hotel Eurostars Residenza Cannaregio, was a convent.

Budget-friendly: For a reasonable price, stay at the Venice Maggior Consiglio, a cozy boutique hotel located only two minutes from Santa Lucia train station.

- **Dorsoduro**

The university neighborhood of Dorsoduro in Venice is crowded with students day and night, giving it a lively and entertaining environment. This area also offers a wealth of amazing cultural attractions.

For everyone who likes art, the Gallerie dell'Accademia museum in Dorsoduro is ideal. This well-known gallery has works by Venetian painters throughout the ages. Additionally, you may go to the renowned Peggy Guggenheim Collection, a private collection of contemporary art gathered by the American heiress who spent a lot of time living in Venice.

The Basilica of San Sebastiano, where Venetian artist Paolo Veronese fled to avoid allegations of murder, is another must-see. He sent the church creative gifts that are still in the building as a token of gratitude for sheltering him. Additionally, the stunning Santa Maria della Salute Basilica, which commands a view of the Grand Canal and the glories of San Marco beyond, is impossible to miss.

Although Dorsoduro is less pricey than the majority of other sections of Venice, if you want to treat yourself, there are several opulent alternatives here. "Best for: People who like art, young professionals, and a lively nightlife".

Lodges close to Dorsoduro

Luxury: On the banks of the Grand Canal, a charming 4-star boutique hotel called Hotel Palazzo Stern offers a breakfast buffet.

Mid-Range: Hotel Ca' Nobile Corner, a 3-star boutique hotel housed in a palace from the fourteenth century.

Budget: The stunning boutique hotel Domus Cavanis is only 350 feet from the Galleria dell'Accademia.

- **Lido**

Long Island Lido in the Venetian lagoon is ideal for a leisurely beach day. Lido's miles-long beaches and breathtaking vistas make it even more appealing. Who wouldn't want to live near a beach? But beachgoers are not the only visitors to Lido. You must explore the numerous breathtaking sights in this region. If you've heard of Lord Byron and want to see where this renowned author of English poetry worked, visit the monastery at San Lazzaro.

A protected natural reserve with a varied environment is called the Oasis of Alberoni. To explore all this sanctuary has to offer, you may hire a bike. Another important historical site is the Church of San Nicola Al Lido. The annual Sposalizio del Mare was held there.

The Doge of Venice marries the city to the Adriatic Sea in a ceremony called Sposalizio del Mare, which translates as "Marriage of the Sea" in English. Everything is symbolic except from when the Doge plunges a gold ring into the water.

The beaches in Lido are what draw visitors in with their wide, unending bodies of water and fine, golden sand. You must take the water bus, which might take some time, to get to Venice's principal attractions.

Lido is a tiny island, thus lodging there may be rather expensive. For everyone who desires a luxurious beach holiday, there are several wonderful luxury hotels available. There are, however, several great solutions in the mid-range and on a budget. "Best for: Beach bums and movie buffs".

Lodging Near Lido

Luxurious: 5-star hotel Ausonia Hungaria Wellness & Lifestyle, surrounded by works of art.

Mid-Range: Hotel Riviera Venezia Lido, a 3-star establishment housed in a former palace and offering sweeping views of the lagoon.

Budget: 3-star Hotel Rivamare is only 66 steps from the beach.

- **Giudecca**

Away from the bustle of the major districts, Giudecca is a developing area of the Venetian lagoon. Giudecca is the ideal destination if you want a location to stay with fewer visitors, a calmer tempo, and a sophisticated nightlife scene. Here, you may sample wines at the surrounding bacari (bars) before going to a casual restaurant to sample some regional specialties.

Additionally, the region is home to numerous breathtaking attractions. The Chiesa Della Zitelle and the Chiesa di Sant'Eufemia are two noteworthy churches that you may visit. The two were constructed in the 16th century by well-known Venetian architect Andrea Palladio. The lagoon in Giudecca is illuminated by fireworks as the Venetians celebrate the Feast of the Redeemer every year on July 14.

Since Giudecca is mostly a residential region, there aren't as many lodging alternatives there. However, several of Venice's renowned 5-star hotels, such as the Belmond Hotel Cipriani, may be found here."Best for People seeking a tranquil neighborhood with opulent alternatives".

Lodges close to Giudecca

Luxury: Belmond Hotel Cipriani is a five-star hotel with breathtaking views of the lagoon.

Mid-range: The 5-star Hilton Molino Stucky Venice has Venice's biggest ballroom and spa.

Budget: The lovely 3-star Hotel Giudecca Venezia, offers breathtaking views of the Palada Canal.

Purchases in Venice

Venetian shopping might be frustrating. The good news is that a few hidden jewels are offering Venice-made goods, from glass to shoes to lace, strewn across the city. Let's find them.

- **Glass and Masks**

Masks and glass are two of the most well-liked and exquisite products available for purchase in Venice. Finding quality is more difficult than you may think. The majority of stores seem to offer subpar Chinese knockoffs, but if you look closely and know where to search, you may still get the genuine article. You may discover information on Casin dei Nobili, the charming tiny shop, which will be of use to you. As soon as I enter Casin dei Nobili, I have the impression that I've entered an amazing Aladdin's cave. I can spend hours in here, much to my husband's chagrin.

- **Markets**

Markets may sometimes reveal a city's spirit; Venice is a good example of this in many ways. Young and elderly meet for a lively glimpse of Venice before the tourist invasion as Venetians continue to swarm the booths and streets around them. On the day of the market, it seems that older people meet together with their old acquaintances from nearby areas and catch up on the newest rumors. While exuberant kids and dogs rush about, attempting (not to) trip everyone, housewives barter with stall owners. Which markets are the best? My favorite ones are these:

Rialto: The Rialto market is the best in Venice for pure vitality and color, and it also boasts the best location of any market in the world. A morning ritual has been taking place here, under the Rialto Bridge, for over a thousand years. The barges arrive at daybreak, and as they unload, a whole commotion of screaming, laughing, and laborious work ensues. Although everything seems chaotic to me, there is order in the chaos, and the market is open for business by six in the morning.

To enjoy it, be sure to arrive early. Several little bars near the market open at the same time as the market or even earlier; they are ideal for getting a quick breakfast of espresso or cappuccino and a delectable pastry before conquering the market. This is the greatest market in the city for purchasing seafood, veggies, or fruit. Therefore, stock up on supplies for your stay if you are self-catering.

Market of the Robes of the Sea: This market on Via Garibaldi in the Castello District is one of the ones I like the best. Although Via Garibaldi is a wonderful street with interesting businesses, the market is the ultimate icing on the cake. It only takes place in October, on the Venice Marathon weekend. If you're already here, the many kiosks offering antiques and strange knickknacks are a terrific place to pick up a one-of-a-kind keepsake.

Market of San Maurizo: This market at Campo San Maurizio, which takes place four or five times a year, is the finest one in Venice for antiques. Despite being written in Italian, the dates are visible on the right side of the page.

Upscale stores: Head to Calle delle Mercerie or Calle Larga XXII Marzo, however, if you're like the majority of Italians and require designer clothing just as much as your daily spaghetti. Both offer enough pricey designer stores to satiate even the most desperate designer soul and are close to St. Mark's Square.

- **Shoes, Flags, and Bags**

Shopping in Venice for leather goods? They seem to be sold at every other store. Most bags are produced in China, with the final assembly taking place in Italy so that a produced in Italy label may be applied.

Bags: Visit Balducci Borse in Cannaregio 1593 to get genuine Made in Italy bags. For years, Franco has made bags by hand in his little workshop and sold them in his tiny store. These are not just ordinary bags; they are also artistic creations and labor of love.

Shoes: Venice is home to a few top-notch shoe boutiques. Try the famous Gabriele Gmeiner in

Campiello del Sol, San Polo 951, for handcrafted men's dress shoes. It takes a small little path to get to this tiny little store/workroom, which is tucked away in a tiny little square. It is most likely difficult to locate.

Do you want a pair of Venetian slippers?
Pay a visit to Piedàterre in 60 S. Polo, Rialto. Enveloping your feet in silk and floating on air is how the slippers feel. They also make a few fashionable bags of excellent quality and are popular with the locals. Don't give it a second thought since the bags sell out very soon. Buy anything right away if you find something you like. The next day, it will no longer exist.

Flags: Venetian flags are sold everywhere, but avoid purchasing the low-quality replicas that begin to fade and come apart as soon as you get them home. Instead, go to A. Santi di Moschini in Castello, Calle delle Bande 5276; their flags are authentic and of the highest quality, and if you're searching for anything in particular, they're also really friendly and informed.

- **Lace**

Only a short boat ride from Venice lies Burano, a vibrant tiny island known for its lace. It's worth going merely to view the colorful fishermen's homes and take in the ambiance, which is quite different from Venice. You will be in lace nirvana here if you like fine lace. They have been honing their methods for more than 500 years, and the lace they produce is the greatest in the world. Even better, Piazza Galupi is home to an excellent lace museum. They can create whatever you need out of lace. Some of the demands they get may shock you.

Although it is pricey, Martina Vidal in Via San Mauro 309 is one of the most renowned stores for shopping. There are several additional small businesses and studios, but anything real and manufactured in the area will be expensive. The pricing is fair, especially considering that everything is handcrafted and of the highest quality.

- **Books**

You must visit the Acqua Alta bookshop in 5167/B Sestiere Castello for an experience like no other. This is an amazing experience, not a bookshop. You get the impression that you have gone down a rabbit hole into Wonderland. Books may be found anywhere. They number thousands. They are stacked from floor to ceiling in a gondola and bathtubs. Cats who have been fed properly snooze leisurely on bookshelves as a canal licks at the door.

You need to go yourself; I can't fully express it. If you go, I ask that you support this Venetian institution by purchasing a book, any book. The greatest place to buy English books is by far Wellington Books on Calle de la Mandola. They provide a great collection of English-language books, ranging from old classics to current top sellers.

- **The shanty**

Time Magazine lists the ghetto of Venice as "one of the world's 100 most important places". But it's not only significant historically; it's also a terrific area to buy, and there aren't many visitors here. *Antichità Al Ghetto*, located at 1133 Cannaregio on the ghetto's periphery, is one of my favorite little art galleries and antique stores in the area. The ghetto is home to several excellent delicatessens and bakeries that are brimming with delicious delights. I guarantee you won't regret spending a morning here.

- **For the Kids**

The boat business owned by Gilberto Penzo is located in San Polo 2681, Calle Seconda dei Saoneri, 30125, and is a great place for boys and parents to buy toys. Gilberto creates the most amazing scale replicas of gondolas and other typical Venetian boats; each one is a one-of-a-kind piece of woodcarving art. Additionally, he offers DIY kits (which my kid adores) and little wooden boats packaged in bottles.

Tips on Where to Eat in Venice Like a Local

There are numerous delectable foods to sample during your vacation to Venice, a city with a rich culinary culture. It might be difficult to locate genuine indigenous food, however, with so many eateries catering to visitors.

The Best Ways to Experience Authentic Food in Venice Despite the City's High Tourist Density Venice offers a variety of real cuisine experiences that are well-liked by residents despite its touristic reputation. Here are some suggestions to assist you in locating the top restaurants in Venice.

1. Steer clear of St. Mark's Square or areas nearby while dining

So where can you sample Venetian food like a local? Restaurants in Piazza San Marco and the neighborhood are sometimes expensive and geared toward visitors. Explore different parts of the city to find cheaper restaurants and more genuine food.

2. Opt for Less Touristy Locations

Local eateries may be found in greater numbers and less touristic locales like Cannaregio, Dorsoduro, and Castello. Look for eateries that are bustling with people as you stroll through these neighborhoods.

3. Select a small and standard restaurant

Small, characteristic eateries called "osterie" or "Bacardi" (wine bars) are excellent locations to sample regional food. These little eateries often have a small menu, but the foods they do offer are flavorful and crafted with fresh, local ingredients. Try squid ink pasta (or squid ink spaghetti), for instance!

4. Sample the regional specialties, such as Cicchetti

We cannot discuss Venetian cuisine without mentioning the characteristic cicchetti, sometimes known as "Venetian tapas." They are a well-known local delicacy and are tiny, bite-sized nibbles that are often served in "Bacardi". They may be eaten as a light supper with a glass of wine or spritz or as a pre-dinner snack. Around the Rialto Bridge neighborhood, you may discover several common places for a reasonable price.

5. Request endorsements

Asking for restaurant suggestions from locals is nothing to be frightened of. We'll probably be delighted to share their favorite eateries and delicacies with you. Finding the finest restaurants in Venice may be difficult despite the city's abundance of wonderful local cuisine.

6. Seek for eateries that include Venetian specialties on the menu

Many eateries in Venice provide typical Italian fare that is available everywhere and appeal to visitors. Look for eateries with a focus on Venetian food and a menu that includes regional favorites like seafood risotto, spaghetti alle vongole, or sarde in saor.

7. Browse local markets and grocery stores

Venetian delicacies and fresh, regionally produced products may be found at Venice's many local markets and dining establishments. Pick up some fresh food, cheese, or cured meats for a picnic at the Mercato di San Polo or the Rialto Market.

8. Sample the local alcoholic beverages

Prosecco, Soave, and Amarone are just a few of the wines and spirits produced in and around Venice. With your meals, be sure to taste some regional wines and spirits like limoncello or grappa.

9. Dine like a local at an Osteria (tavern in Italian) in the area.

Osterias are informal, family-run eateries that specialize in serving traditional Italian food. Look for taverns in the city's more residential neighborhoods, and don't be shy about chatting with the waitstaff or other patrons to seek their advice on what to order.

CHAPTER 5

Visiting the Areas of Venice

The Contemporary Mainland: Mestre

Mestre is what and where?

By rail and vehicle bridges across the lagoon, Mestre is the mainland town that is linked to Venice. Although we don't advise it, some travelers choose to stay there as a less expensive alternative to Venice. Mestre is everything that Venice isn't: contemporary, nasty, congested, and every day. Administratively, it is a suburb of Venice (Venezia), kind of. It does, however, have a distinct history and personality from other towns.

History

Mestre has a long history, although it has always been overshadowed by its mighty neighbor Venice. The defenses here were fought over, captured, destroyed, and rebuilt throughout the centuries-long fighting and quarreling that raged across mainland Italy. Unlike Venice, it did not have a lagoon to defend it. The town continued to be vulnerable to enemy invasions even after Venice had control of it in the fourteenth century.

Mestre lost its distinct identity as a town in the 1920s when it was incorporated into the Comune di Venezia. However, Mestre found itself becoming a center for migrants while losing administrative authority. To enhance the local economy, a sizable port and industrial complex was built in Porto Marghera throughout the 1920s and 1930s. Mestre, which is next door, expanded as workers from all over Italy came and needed a place to reside. As local Venetians chose to relocate across the sea, the 1960s and 1970s saw a fast expansion. There may not have been any planning oversight of the unsightly residential and industrial constructions popping up all over Mestre since it was still run from Venice. Over 200,000 people now live there. In modern times, the town has sought to forge a stronger sense of its own identity, but to outsiders, it remains a cruel residential twin to the nearby Porto Marghera, the industrial port complex that so horrifies the newcomer to Venice.

These days, the population of this conurbation on the mainland is over three times that of Venice, an island. In essence, Mestre offered—and continues to offer—the type of life that many Italians want. They may live in contemporary homes or flats with room for their kids to play. They can ride bicycles or drive vehicles. They left their gloomy, dark apartments, which were in danger from increasing dampness and high water, in their hundreds, and chose the exciting new world of contemporary Mestre. Additionally, there were opportunities available in the crowded industrial ports. The flow is now reversed during the daytime, with many of Venice's employees—including her gondoliers—commuting daily from Mestre. If you are at Piazzale Roma in the early morning, you will see them; a large number of native Venetians disembarking from buses and making their way along those annoying canals to work in hotels, gift shops, and restaurants to support the rapidly growing tourism industry that has all but taken over Venice.

Shopping

You won't have many reasons to visit Mestre if you remain on or call the island of Venice home. The town doesn't have many attractions, however, you may go through it on the train. Shopping is the main exception to this. Mestre has typical businesses with typical costs. Even though there are now supermarkets and commercial shops in Venice, Mestre often has superior selections.

Centro Le Barche, a relatively new retail center in Mestre, is the best place to go shopping. If you need to inexpensively restock your baggage, the H&M clothing shop inside is perfect. There is a sizable Coin department store, a supermarket, and a huge Feltrinelli bookstore with a travel area and English-language publications. Even the restrooms in the mall are free, which is unheard of in Venice.

From the retail center, a small pedestrian street leads to Piazza Ferretto. There are additional inexpensive stores selling clothing, underwear, and other items along this route and under the portico of the plaza. One of these stores is a Sephora branch.

Near Mestre

The town's central plaza, Piazza Ferretto, is Mestre's most alluring feature. If you've only heard negative things about Mestre, you may be surprised by how big, long, and gorgeous this is. There are cafés where you may pass the time in the day, together with a welcoming crowd. The pedestrian-only area is surrounded by remarkable and ancient structures, notably the Chiesa di San Lorenzo, the town's most significant church, which dates back to the seventeenth century. The main landmark of Mestre is the Torre Civica, a rebuilt clock tower that was formerly a part of the town's medieval walls and is also known as the Torre dell'Orologio. A few sections of arcaded streets that are further historical relics of the town may be found beyond the tower. Near the Venetian lagoon's edge is a much more recent attraction. A brand-new public park with trees, walkways, and views of the lagoon, Parco San Giuliano, was constructed on the former wasteland. The Heineken Jammin' Festival was held there in 2007, however, it was abruptly canceled due to an unusual storm. Although there is discussion of a museum in the future, Mestre does not currently have any other significant tourist attractions.

Venetians can go to Mestre for entertainment and nightlife in addition to shopping. Here, there are additional possibilities, including several movie theaters and nightclubs. If you're thinking about going out late at night to dance, do your homework and make sure you have transportation arranged; some events are out of the way and can only be reached by automobile.

Getting from Mestre to Venice

Buses running between Mestre and Venice often cross the Ponte della Liberta Lagoon Bridge to get to Piazzale Roma, Venice's bus terminal. Between the plaza and the Grand Canal, there is an information kiosk operated by ACTV where you may purchase tickets and obtain instructions. A convenient service is bus number 4, which travels over the bridge, turns right into Mestre along the straight Corso del Popolo, and passes Piazza 27 Ottobre, where you may get off to visit Le Barche retail center and the center of town.

In the event of traffic issues, the railway line from Venice passes Mestre station and is a helpful detour (traffic incidents may shut down the road bridge into Venice for hours). However, since Mestre's station is close to the town's center, buses are often more practical.

Travel choices to Mestre

Mestre has strong transportation options; almost all buses and trains that go between Venice and the rest of Italy stop here. For Mestre beside the station, the ATVO Ryanair bus from Treviso Airport often stops (ask the driver), as does their service for Cortina d'Ampezzo in the Dolomites. The Mestre station is within a short distance from the Venice Marco Polo Airport, and there are inexpensive ACTV urban buses (number 15 to Mestre railway station and number 5 into Venice via Parco San Giuliano) as well as a direct ATVO 'Fly Bus' link between the two. If you're staying in Mestre, ask your hotel for instructions since the city is large and difficult to navigate.

Hotels

For travelers on a limited budget, who are anxious to be closer to the airport, or who are planning further travel and require vehicle parking, Mestre has a ton of hotels. However, visitors can expect a different experience from the Venice shown on postcards. If at all possible, we suggest staying in Venice itself.

Islands of Venice

The Venetian Islands are a group of artificial islands in Biscayne Bay, north of Palm Island, Hibiscus Island, and Star Island. They are a part of Miami and Miami Beach. Biscayne Island, San Marco Island, Di Lido Island, San Marino Island, Rivo Alto Island, and Belle Isle are the six islands linked by the Venetian Causeway.

The American Airlines Arena, home of the NBA World Champions Miami Heat, the Adrienne Arsht Center for the Performing Arts, Bayside Marketplace with a wide variety of shops and dining options, and the Port of Miami, which is home to some of the biggest cruise ships in the world, are all easily accessible from Downtown Miami when traveling west on the Venetian Causeway. You may quickly reach the center of the thriving South Beach neighborhood with Lincoln Road between 16th and 17th Streets, which is renowned for its chic boutiques and thrilling nightlife, by traveling east on the Venetian Causeway and exiting on 17th Street. Residents now often stroll, exercise, ride bikes, walk their pets, and watch the sunset on the Venetian Causeway.

The Venetian Islands are home to several magnificent waterfront residences with gorgeous landscaping and ornate furnishings that provide breathtaking views of Biscayne Bay and the Miami cityscape. This tropical paradise has drawn visitors from all over the globe, and the affluent are still drawn there by the chic, tranquil island lifestyle they can retire to regularly.

Tides and a Lagoon

The lagoon has always been essential to Venice's existence. It was created by the combination of Adriatic tidal currents and the waters of various Alpine rivers (Piave, Sile, Bacchiglione, and Brenta). Its mud banks, shallows, and channels support salt pans, as well as marine and avian life. The lagoon has acted as both a natural sewage system, with the tides cleaning away the city's canals twice daily, and as defense (the Venetians overcame the Genoese in 1380 thanks to their better understanding of the navigable channels).

But to keep the lagoon from endangering Venice's very survival, it has to be carefully tended. The Adriatic Sea has risen, the Po River basin has geologically sunk, channels have been deepened in the 20th century, fresh water from mainland aquifers has been over-extracted, and there is a significant flooding issue as a result. Regularly, high tides and winds from the south and east cause the lagoon to rise and flood the city, causing the acqua alta ("high water") that Venetians are so accustomed to. To prevent this from happening, elaborate raised platforms are set up in the city's major squares to allow visitors and other people to walk around the area. In 1966, a particularly bad deluge occurred, sparking several national and even worldwide attempts to investigate the issue and provide remedies. In 1988, engineers started testing a prototype for a mechanical barrage that would be built and lifted in times of floods to shut the lagoon. However, development has been slowed down by overlapping local, regional, and national bureaucratic issues as well as concerns about how ambitious engineering projects may affect the lagoon's biological balance. Although a regional body oversees the Veneto region, which has hydrographic and industrial issues that have a significant impact on the problems of the lagoon and city, Venice has its city council that has final responsibility for the day-to-day operations of the city. Additionally, historical structures, port operations, and museums and galleries are all directly impacted by national government departments. The railroads, the airport, and what is left of the oil and chemical industry situated in Marghera are just a few of the major enterprises that have been nationalized or are partially held by the government. Due to the administrative gridlock caused by these competing powers and conflicts of interest, Venice is still susceptible to flooding and may potentially have a repeat of the tragedy from 1966.

CHAPTER 6

Dynamic Cities in Venice

The Sestieri: The Six Districts of Venice

While other cities have "quarters," Venice refers to its neighborhoods as "sestieri." What are the major activities in each of Venice's sestieri, and how many of them are there? Here is a brief overview of Venice's six districts.

- **San Marco**

The center of Venice and its most recognizable landmarks are found in San Marco, as suggested by the neighborhood's name. There is the Piazza San Marco with its magnificent church and the Doge's Palace. From the "Ponte della Paglia" behind Palazzo Ducale, one can see the renowned "Ponte dei Sospiri," beyond which the Castello neighborhood starts.

The Treasury of San Marco, located within the basilica, the Correr Museum, and the National

Archaeological Museum are just a few of the notable museums in this sestieri. As a result, if you just have a day to spend in Venice, you should concentrate most of your time here.

- **Cannaregio**

The Jewish Museum of Venice, which details the rich history of the neighborhood's Jewish Quarter, is located in Cannaregio, the biggest sestieri in all of Venice. Along with the beautiful Chiesa di Santa Maria degli Scalzi, this area is home to Venice's five medieval synagogues. One of the most astounding palazzi in all of Venice is the 15th-century Cannaregio. This city is famous for its magnificent palazzi, particularly those that border the Grand Canal.

- **San Polo**

The Rialto Market and Campo San Polo, the second-largest plaza in the city after San Marco, are both situated in this more relaxed area of the city, which offers a lot to explore and discover. Despite being the tiniest sestiere in Venice, don't allow its small size to put you off. It is the most abundant at tiny, classic Venetian restaurants known as "bàcari" and artisan stores. This neighborhood is connected to San Marco by the famous Rialto Bridge, making it simple to reach when you wish to explore a bit more sedate neighborhood and sample local wines and nibbles, known as cichéti.

- **Dorsoduro**

Dorsoduro is the Venice sestieri to visit if you're a reader since it has several wonderful bookstores. It is also known for being the city's university district and one of the most vibrant sections of Venice. The Ca' Foscari University and the renowned Peggy Guggenheim Collection are two of the district's attractions and a must-see for art enthusiasts. We have a suggestion for you if all you want to do is take a walk. Visit Campo Santa Margherita, a charming piazza that never sleeps, bustling with students at night and with residents throughout the day.

- **Santa Croce**

Santa Croce has a lot to offer, from the bustling San Giacomo dell'Orio piazza and its ancient cathedral to Venice's interesting Museum of Modern Art. The primary bus station for the city is located in this neighborhood at Piazzale Roma, therefore if you arrive in Venice by bus you may begin your tour of the Venice sestieri from the Santa Croce neighborhood.

- **Castello**

Castello is one of Venice's less crowded neighborhoods, making it a fantastic choice if you want to avoid the throng. The renowned Arsenale, the Naval History Museum, and many other attractions are located there. For additional suggestions on things to see in Castello, check out our guide.

The Venice Grand Canal

The Grand Waterway is Venice's biggest and most well-known waterway. It divides Venice into two halves and is little about four kilometers long. The most significant canal crisscrossing this wonderful city is the Grand Canal of Venice, usually referred to as Canalazzo.

The lovely canals that go through every part of the city like streets are what define Venice the most. The Grand Canal, which divides Venice in two and is four kilometers long, is the longest and most significant of all.

How do you navigate the Grand Canal?
The Grand Canal may be crossed by both tourists and residents using a variety of methods, such as a Water Bus or a Traghetto.

One of the four bridges that span the canal may be used if you wish to walk:

The city's most picturesque and historic bridge is the Rialto Bridge.

Ponte dell' Accademia: In its initial 1854 construction, the Ponte dell' Accademia was made of steel. A wooden building subsequently took its place.

Ponte degli Scalzi: Due to its proximity to the train station, Ponte degli Scalzi, which translates to "the Bridge of the Barefoot," is also known as the Bridge of the Station and the Railway.

The most renowned bridge in Venice, the Ponte della Costituzione, was created by the Spanish architect Santiago Calatrava. It runs from Piazzale Roma to the train station in Venezia Santa Lucia.

Vaporetto along the Grand Canal
The Grand Canal is traversed by the Water Buses, which make stops along both banks of the waterway. It is a wonderful and affordable way to take in the stunning structures and palazzos that are situated on each side of the city's major thoroughfare. Line 1 is the ideal Vaporetto to go around the Grand Canal. The route passes by the Ca' d'Oro Palazzo, Santa Maria della Salute, the Gallerie dell'Accademia, the Palazzo Ca'Rezzonico, and the well-known Rialto Bridge.

Venice's Hidden Gems: Off-the-Beaten-Path

Throughout the year, this city receives visitors from all over the globe, and it never slows down. The popular and hidden treasures of Venice are endless, but there is only so much one can accomplish with limited money and time.

The majority of well-known locations are always crowded and difficult to properly explore. But Venice is much more than the short list of attractions that appear in every guidebook for tourists. Most individuals are unaware that there are locations concealed in plain sight. Here are a few undiscovered treasures that should be on your bucket list if you want to get the most out of your time in Venice.

Palazzo Grimani: You must not miss Venice's "hidden gem," the Palazzo Grimani. The Venetian Bishop Giovanni Grimani's collection of antiques and possessions, a crucial component of Venice's cultural evolution, is housed in this hidden treasure. You would regret missing out on this undiscovered treasure if you didn't visit this gorgeous building, which has magnificent artwork and stunning furnishings.

Scala Contarini del Bovolo: Another lovely undiscovered treasure in Venice is the Scala Contarini del Bovolo, which is located in the San Marco area. One of the most Instagrammable locations in Venice is this spiral staircase, which is a work of art in and of itself. This staircase, which was built in Venice in the Gothic and Renaissance architectural styles, is a little-known treasure that shouldn't be overlooked. The top of the eighty stairs offers a breathtaking perspective of the San Marco neighborhood and all of its exquisite Venetian architecture. Given that not many people are aware of this stairway, it is one of the most enjoyable hidden attractions in Venice to discover.

San Zaccaria's Flooded Crypt: One of the many beautiful churches in Venice is the church of San Zaccaria. Both the stunning interior and the stunning exterior of this Renaissance-style building make it a must-see location. However, the crypt that is tucked under the church is the location that visitors often miss. The grave of the church's namesake is located in this partially submerged crypt. It is strongly recommended that you go into the crypt and explore it, even trying to walk on water, for a small price of 1.5 Euros. One of Venice's most intriguing and adventurous hidden jewels, this one allows you to get up close to the past.

Campo San Margherita: Campo Santa Margherita is a hidden treasure in Venice and should be on your list if you want to appreciate the calmer side of the city without the crowds of visitors and lengthy lines. Even the locals come here to avoid the crowds since it is the ideal location to do so. A flea market selling goods made in the area can be found during the day, and at night, the palazzo is inhabited by the local student population, who can be seen having a good time drinking and chatting. If you want to get away from the crowds and have some relaxation, this is the hidden treasure you should check out.

San Giorgio Maggiore: You should take a day excursion to the island of San Giorgio Maggiore to see this stunning undiscovered attraction in Venice. The chapel on the island was painted by Monet and was constructed in 1566. It is lovely to see and explore. The building's hues stand out even more in the blue seas that surround the island, which provides for some stunning photos. You may also explore the just-opened wooden labyrinth created as a monument to the Argentinian author Jorge Luis Borges. Another feature of this undiscovered treasure that must not be overlooked is the bell tower. This bell tower, which is reachable by a glass elevator, offers some of the most stunning views of Venice. This is a hidden treasure in Venice and ought to be on your list.

Ca'Macana: Since ancient times, the mask has been a staple of Venetian fashion, and it has endured the test of time. Masks are still worn by Venetians as part of their fashion sense. At Ca'Macana, which has been producing distinctive masks for a very long time, this heritage may be studied in further detail. This undiscovered treasure is claimed to have connections to luminaries like Kubrick and the city's famous opera venues. Visit this undiscovered treasure, and take one of the courses they offer to learn the craft of producing masks.

Doge's Palace Tours with Secret Routes: Anyone visiting Venice should include a trip to the iconic Doge's Palace, but most visitors are unaware that there is a tour available that takes you to areas normally off-limits to the general public. This is the exclusive Secret Itineraries excursion, which requires reservations. On this trip, you are escorted inside the chambers that are off-limits to the general public and get the opportunity to get up close and personal with intriguing and significant elements of Venetian history. The Chamber of the Inquisitors, the

Chamber of the Three Head Magistrates, the Chamber of the Hidden Chancellery, etc. are some examples of the hidden chambers. The jail cells where the renowned Cassanova was held captive are also accessible. If you reserve a trip in advance, this hidden treasure will remain well-kept and will be worthwhile.

Ponte di Chiodo and Ponte di Diavolo, often known as "The Bridge without a Parapet,"
Only two of Venice's more than 400 bridges still lack parapets, out of the city's total number of bridges. The first one is called the Ponte di Chiodo and is situated in the Cannaregio neighborhood of Venice. It was formerly owned by the Chiodo family.

The Ponte di Diavolo, so called from a proverb about the devil, is the second bridge, also in the Laguna Veneta region. Without the interruption of people, you may stroll over these bridges in total safety and snap breathtaking pictures. When visiting Venice, you should include these undiscovered jewels on your itinerary since they are must-see destinations.

Isola Di San Michele: One of Venice's undiscovered beauties, the Isola Di San Michele is one of the lagoon's less-traveled islands. Despite not being a conventional tourist destination, it is nonetheless worthwhile to visit. The island is referred to as Venice's graveyard since it is home exclusively to churches and extensive lanes of graves. San Michele may be a peaceful retreat from the bustle of Venice where you can visit the several lovely cemeteries and explore the churches. This peaceful hidden treasure is the ideal change of scenery from the raucous hordes of Venice.

Libreria Acqua Alta: This Venice treasure is straight out of a fairy film. The Libreria Acqua Alta serves as a spot where tourists are reminded that Venice truly floats on water. You may explore and purchase both new and old books at the library or bookshop. The owner stores the books in vintage bathtubs, canoes, barrels, and even gondolas—yes, the ones you see floating about the city. The staircase built of used books, which sticks out, is another item to see. The lovers of books and photographers will both like this Venice hidden treasure.

Scuola Grande Di San Marco: The Scuola Grande di San Marco, which was formerly a school, is now a municipal hospital in the San Marco neighborhood. However, this metropolitan hospital has a mystery tucked away above it. There is a stairway that ascends to a room that serves as the Museum of the History of Medicine, which is situated directly above the hospital and is open to the public for free admission. This museum is a fantastic hidden treasure that you should see the next time you are in Venice since not many people are aware of it. You may browse and explore the museum's collection of intriguing items, which includes old medical relics, books, and other trinkets.

Isola Della Certosa: Another island that is mostly unexplored by tourists is Isola Della

Certosa, making it one of the greatest secret spots in Venice to avoid the throng. This hidden location is the ideal place for you to unwind in the gardens or have some fun in the water after seeing all the old structures and architecture. The huge park located in Certosa offers breathtaking views of Venice and the Venetian lagoon as well as opportunities to picnic and play activities. After long days of touring, it might be pleasant to engage in some water activities nearby. You must include this undiscovered treasure on your list of Venice's must-see attractions.

Innate San Francesco Della Vigna: San Francesco Della Vigna is a secret treasure of Venice that you should not miss if you like the serenity and calm that stillness gives. Since this church is also a monastery and is situated at the very edge of the city, visitors are required to keep quiet. You may gaze at the exquisite murals and frescoes that adorn the church's interior. You may also tour the church's grounds, where you'll discover amazing-looking orange trees. This serene hidden treasure is a location that must be on your list.

The Basilica of the Salute: The Basilica Della Salute is the place to go if you like music and would want to listen to some Venetian-style music. The music is wonderful and there are daily public organ concertos here. Your next trip to Venice should surely include a stop to this hidden treasure.

CHAPTER 7

Learning About Venetian Culture

Unearthing the Vibrant Arts and Crafts of Venice: from Glassblowing to Gondola Making

Enter the lovely city of Venice and get ready to be mesmerized by its extensive creative legacy. This floating city is a hidden gem of arts and crafts that are just waiting to be discovered. It is well known for its complex glassblowing skills and famous gondolas.

Venice is a refuge for artists and craftspeople, from the well-known Murano glass factory to the charming enterprises nestled away in the winding alleyways. Each piece of glassblowing art radiates incomparable beauty and timelessness thanks to decades of careful creative development. But Venice is alive with more than simply glass.

The city also has a vibrant heritage of creating gondolas, where talented artisans painstakingly construct each boat, making sure that every aspect is ideal. No two gondolas are similar, making each one a one-of-a-kind piece of art, from the delicate carvings on the oarlocks to the polished woodwork.

Join us as we explore Venice's thriving arts and crafts sector and learn about the stories of creativity and craftsmanship that have defined this magnificent city. Get ready to be moved and impressed by the skill and creativity that Venice is home to.

Modern Glass: While some of the most notable glass stores and galleries may be found in the city of Venice, Murano is the island known for its glass manufacturers.

Lace Burano: Burano is an island in the Venetian Lagoon famous for its vibrant buildings, but it is also home to the traditional craft of lace.

The Pure Gold leaf and the Gold Beater: The oldest artisan techniques. One of the oldest crafts being practiced today in Venice is the gilding of wood with pure gold leaf.

The Squeraroli; the Gondola and the Squeri's history": The Builders' History of the Gondolas. The original Venetian Gondola was created in the Squero, and the Squeraroli are craftsmen skilled in creating these well-known rowing boats of the Adriatic Lagoon, also known as the Gondolas.

Venetian goldsmithing: a historical overview and exemplary jewelry, including the Moretto of Venice. Learn about the interesting history of Venetian jewelry and its distinctive cultural heritage by visiting the website for the Venetian goldsmiths. Examine the filigree and other defining features of Venetian goldsmithing.

Venetian Festivals and Celebrations: Their Allure

A Special Combination of Tradition and Celebration

In the historically and culturally rich city of Venice, the past is not only remembered but also fervently honored. This is shown by the city's festivals and festivities, each of which is a colorful display that brings Venetian customs to life in an enthralling manner.

Each festival, from the spectacular masks and costumes of the Venice Carnevale to the somber processions of the Festa della Sensa, is a unique fusion of modern art, festivity, and tradition. They serve as a showcase for Venice's rich cultural legacy and serve as an active demonstration of the traditions and practices that have molded the city's character throughout time.

These activities are not simply for show; they are interwoven in the social fabric of the city. They serve as an occasion for Venetians to unite, celebrate their common history and culture, and carry on these customs to the next generation. They serve as a constant reminder of the city's resilient character and a demonstration of its capacity for change while maintaining its identity.

The Contribution of Festivals and Celebrations to Tourism in Venice

The city's tourist business greatly benefits from the festivals and festivities that take place in Venice. They provide visitors with an opportunity to explore the city outside of the typical tourist routes, making them a significant appeal for visitors. These activities provide a unique and immersive approach to seeing the city, taking part in its customs, and feeling a connection to its rich cultural past.

These occasions provide a chance for the discerning tourist to see Venice from the perspective of its inhabitants. They provide an opportunity to experience the city's spirit, partake in its customs, and create lifelong memories. These festivals provide a unique and memorable Venetian experience, whether it's taking in the huge spectacle of the Carnevale, taking part in the historical reenactments of the Festa della Sensa, or taking in the cultural extravaganza of the Biennale.

However, it's not just about the show. In addition to bringing in people from all over the globe, these events have a big impact on the local economy by bringing in money for companies there. They are an essential component of the city's tourist sector, supporting the regional economy and safeguarding the city's cultural history for the next generations.

Therefore, the city's festivals and festivities are a must-see whether you're an experienced tourist searching for a distinctive cultural experience or a first-time visitor hoping to discover a different side of Venice. They honor Venice's history, highlight its lively culture, and serve as evidence of the city's lasting allure.

Please be aware that certain festivals' dates may change every year, so it's always a good idea to check their official websites or local listings for the most up-to-date information.

Important Festivals & Holidays in Venice

- **Venice's Most Famous Festival is Carnevale**

The Carnevale di Venezia, or Venice Carnival, is one of the world's most celebrated and joyful events. Every year, the floating city welcomes thousands of costumed revelers to partake in the festivities. There is no shortage of entertainment, including gondola rides, extravagant processions, masquerade parties, and street festivals.

The Venice Carnival is held every year in February or March, with the precise dates varying from year to year. The carnival will take place from February 15 to March 4 this year. From the beginning of Lent until Ash

Wednesday, the Carnival of Venice traditionally lasts 18 days.

The Venice Carnival has a long history, beginning in the 12th century as a means for Venetians to have fun and relax before the 40-day Lenten fast. Carnival continues to be a time when people may let their cares go and have fun while enjoying music, dancing, and parades.

The event was appealing because it provided influential individuals an opportunity to act out without thinking about their reputations. They partied hard at wild parties, orgies, and gambling dens while remaining anonymous behind elaborate carnival masks.

The Venice Carnival now resembles a historical recreation one could see at a Renaissance fair. Locals and visitors congregate around the canals as elaborately dressed figures, savoring Venetian specialties, free live performances, and entertainment.

- **Festa della Sensa: An Ancient Water Festival**

Each year, on the Sunday after Ascension Day, Venice hosts the Festa della Sensa, a traditional festival. This festival honors two important historical occurrences in the city: the symbolic union of the city with the sea and the suppression of an uprising in Dalmatia in the year 1000 AD.

The Doge (Venetian monarch), who symbolizes marriage, ceremonially throws a gold ring into the Adriatic Sea. This deed expresses Venice's control over the water and its appreciation for the wealth of the sea that has blessed the city.

Both residents and visitors enjoy the distinctive spectacle of the Festa della Sensa. A water procession including the Serenissima, a recreation of the Doge's ship from the sixteenth century, kicks off the festival. The "wedding" ceremony is held at the Port of San Nicol, where the procession departs from San Marco. The

Sensa Market at the Church of San Nicol and the Venetian rowing championship competitions take place after the ceremony.

Traveling to Venice during the Festa della Sensa provides a rare chance to experience a custom that has been woven into the city's cultural heritage for many years. It's an opportunity to see Venice in a new way, where the past and current coexist in a lovely festival on the river.

The Festa della Sensa's date changes every year since it is determined by the liturgical calendar. It often takes place on the Sunday that follows Ascension Day (40 days after Easter).

- **Festa del Redentore: Thanksgiving in Venice**

One of the most passionate festivities for Venetians is the Festa del Redentore, also known as the Feast of the Redeemer, which is eagerly awaited by visitors. This celebration, which takes place on the third weekend in July, honors the cessation of the plague that ravaged Venice in the sixteenth century.

A third of Venice's population perished due to the plague, and in 1576 Doge Alvise Mocenigo II pledged to build a chapel if it subsided. A temporary bridge linking Zattere and the Redentore Church is constructed each year for this celebration. The Redentore Church was constructed on the Giudecca island.

The two-day Festa del Redentore is a religious celebration involving activities and fireworks. Venetians hang lanterns and balloons from their boats and the city's canals on Saturday. As dusk sets, a magnificent fireworks show illuminates the sky over St. Mark's Basin and reflects on the lake below. A night of celebrations with parties on the decked-out boats and beside the canals follows.

A somber religious procession is held on Sunday. People cross across to the Redentore Church to attend services when the makeshift bridge of boats is opened. The Redentore Regattas, a series of competitive boat races, bring the festival to a close.

You may get a sense of Venice's lengthy history and its residents' tenacity by taking part in the Festa del Redentore. It is an expression of appreciation, vitality, and the city's ongoing connection with the sea.

- **Regata Storica: The Classic Boat Race of Venice**

One of the most eagerly awaited festivals in Venice, the Regata Storica, turns Venice's Grand Canal into a lively spectacle every first Sunday of September. A throwback to a period when Venice was a significant maritime force, the historical Regatta boat races pay homage to the city's rich nautical legacy.

The event begins with a magnificent procession of boats designed to resemble those from the 16th century being rowed by gondoliers wearing historical attire. Of course, the series of boat races that come next are the highlight. The most thrilling of them is the "Campioni su Gondolini" race, in which gondoliers fight against one another in small, quick gondola boats. It is quite amazing to see these slick boats gliding across the Grand Canal while being cheered on by passionate crowds.

Did you realize? One of the oldest customs in Venice, the Regata Storica dates back to the middle of the thirteenth century!

If you're thinking of coming at this time, be sure to reserve a good viewing location in advance. Most people choose to watch the race from the Rialto Bridge or the Grand Canal banks, but for a really unique experience, think about taking a gondola trip. Just make sure you reserve early!

The Regata Storica is not just a race; it's a celebration of Venice's enduring love affair with the sea. It's a chance to witness a tradition that has been kept alive for centuries, a testament to the city's resilience and its people's unwavering spirit.

- **Biennale di Venezia: A Cultural Extravaganza**

The Biennale di Venezia is a world-renowned cultural event that takes place every two years in Venice, hence the name "Biennale". It's a must-visit for any art enthusiast as it is a very significant international art exhibition that brings in many of the world's greatest contemporary artists.

The Biennale di Venezia is divided into several sectors, including Art, Architecture, Cinema, Dance, Music, and Theatre. Each sector hosts its own special events, exhibitions, and performances, turning the entire city into a vibrant cultural hub. The Art and Architecture sectors are particularly noteworthy, attracting artists, architects, and critics from around the globe.

Did you know? The first Biennale di Venezia was held in 1895, making it one of the oldest and most prestigious cultural events in the world!

The Biennale Art, also known as the Venice Art Biennale, is one of the most prestigious contemporary art exhibitions in the world. It usually takes place from May to November and features works from artists representing various countries. Each country has its own national pavilion, showcasing the best of their contemporary art scene.

The Biennale Architecture, on the other hand, is a major event in the field of architecture. It's a platform where architects and designers can exchange ideas and showcase their works. It usually takes place in the odd years, alternating with the Art Biennale.

If you're planning to attend the Biennale di Venezia, make sure to check the official website for the latest updates and schedules. And don't forget to explore other things to do in Venice while you're there!

- **An International Film Festival, the Venice Film Festival**

One of the longest-running and most renowned film festivals in the world is the Venice Film Festival, also known as Mostra Internazionale d'Arte Cinematografica di Venezia. It has been a mainstay of Venice's cultural landscape since its founding in 1932 and is a component of the Venice Biennale.

On the picturesque island of Lido, the event is often held in late August or early September in the famed Palazzo del Cinema on the Lungomare Marconi. Any fan of movies should go there, and the Venice Film Festival attracts the most famous people outside of Carnival.

The renowned Golden Lion Award, presented at the Venice Film Festival to the finest film exhibited there, is well-known. It has been given to some of the most important movies and directors in cinema history throughout the years.

Did you realize? The oldest film festival in the world is the Venice Film Festival, which debuted in 1932.

The festival's purpose is to increase awareness and promote world film in all of its forms as art, entertainment, and as an industry in a spirit of freedom and conversation. It is officially recognized by the FIAPF (World Federation of Film Producers Association).

Make sure to visit the official website of the Venice Film Festival for the most recent schedules and changes if you want to attend. Also, don't miss other fantastic films using Venice as their setting! It certainly makes you feel like visiting this lovely city.

- **San Marco Festival: Celebrating Venice's Patron Saint**

In Venice's cultural calendar, the Festa di San Marco, often known as St. Mark's Feast, is a prominent occasion. In honor of Saint Mark, the patron saint of Venice, it is celebrated every year on April 25. This day is not just a time for religious observance; it is also a time to celebrate Venetian history and pride.

There are religious processions, musical performances, and celebrations during the Festa di San Marco. A large procession to St. Mark's Basilica, where a special liturgy is conducted, is the major attraction. The major gathering place for the celebrations is the Piazza San Marco, which bears the saint's name in Venice.

Did you realize? After his relics were reputedly taken from Alexandria by Venetian traders in the ninth century and transported to Venice, St. Mark was named the patron saint of Venice.

The Festa di San Marco is well-known for the traditional "Bocolo" custom in addition to its religious components. On this day, Venetian men express their love and respect for the ladies in their lives by giving them a "Bocolo"—a single red rosebud.

If you decide to go to Venice during the Festa di San Marco, you'll have the chance to take part in a special mingling of spiritual traditions, regional culture, and romantic traditions.

Venetian Festivals & Celebrations You Should Consider Attending

These minor festivals, although not as widely known as the Venice International Film Festival or Carnival, keep the city buzzing and are enjoyable to attend.

Festa di San Rocco: The Saint's Day Celebration - Saint Roch, the patron saint of plague victims, is honored during the Festa di San Rocco, a Catholic celebration celebrated in Venice. The Church of San Rocco, famous for its breathtaking Tintoretto paintings, hosts a big procession and a special service as part of the celebration on August 16.

Festival of the Lilies - Festa dei Gigli Unknown yet attractive, the Festa dei Gigli, also known as the Festival of Lilies, is held in Venice. It's a celebration of flowers that heralds the coming of spring, with lilies serving as a symbol of innocence and elegance. Although the precise day varies, it usually happens in the spring.

Festa della Madonna della Salute, also known as the Festival of the Madonna of Health, is a religious celebration that takes place on November 21st in Venice. A procession to the Basilica of Santa Maria della Salute for a special liturgy marks the end of a horrific epidemic in 1630.

Children's Celebration of San Martin: Festa di San Martino On November 11th, there is a wonderful kids' celebration called the Festa di San Martino. This day, which honors Saint Martin, is characterized by happiness, sweets, and the sound of youngsters laughing as they march through the streets with lanterns.

Festa del Mosto: Honoring the Harvest - The Festa del Mosto is a customary Venetian celebration honoring the grape harvest and the first pressing of the grapes to produce Mosto, or young wine. On the island of Sant'Erasmo, referred to as Venice's vegetable garden, it often occurs around October.

The top restaurants in Venice

The cuisine options in Venice are unmatched, from Michelin-starred restaurants to very fresh seafood. This city has established a reputation as one of the world's most romantic vacation sites because of its abundance of tranquil places to people-watch, cultural hotspots, and stunning osterias. Venice is unlike any other city and the greatest part? drinking and eating all day long while enjoying views of the river that are unmatched anywhere on the planet.

Naturally, Venice has some of the best cuisine options in the world. All the hallmarks of traditional Italian cuisine are presented here masterfully. Fresh seafood and Venetian meat dishes are available in addition to traditional pasta meals like spaghetti vongole and black tagliolini with cuttlefish ink. No two meals are the same since so many distinct flavors, cooking techniques, and ingredients have been combined here. And that's how things ought to be. The top eateries in Venice are listed below.

Best restaurants in Venice

1. Trattoria al Gatto Nero

One of Venice's best restaurants is located on the island of Burano, which is renowned for its excellent lace-making and vibrant homes. Ruggero and Lucia Bovo, who are husband and wife, introduce "The Black Cat" with a smile, and their very endearing son Massimiliano plays the maitre d'. The family is passionate about eating regional cuisine and helping Burano's declining number of fishermen. Almost all of the food on the menu is netted or manually fished in the lagoon. Try handmade tagliolini with spider crab or traditional Burano risotto with goby fish, two hyper-local delicacies. Thanks to the Bovo family's emphasis on serving locals, this is one of the few upscale restaurants in Venice with diverse customers. Tom Cruise may be your next-door neighbor on one side, and Andrea Rossi, a fourth-generation fisherman who caught the fish in your dish, could be your neighbor on the other. This is the pinnacle of Venice.

2. Restaurant Glitz

Two Michelin stars have been awarded to Ristorante Glam in recognition of Chef Enrico Bartolini's skill in transforming traditional Venetian meals into mouthwatering nibbles. It is located within the Palazzo Venart Hotel and offers outside seating directly under century-old magnolia trees. Spend a few hours eating spaghetti with local mussels and shallots or rice with borage and razor clams by ordering the tasting menu, an exploration of eight flavors unique to the lagoon. Make a reservation well in advance since they are some of the most highly sought-after tables in all of Venice.

3. La Zucca

La Zucca, which means "the pumpkin" in Italian, is a cozy restaurant with a cuisine unlike any other in Venice. The rotating menu, which is updated daily, emphasizes vegetables; don't miss the famous pumpkin and ricotta flan. It also has delectable specialties like roasted rabbit with chestnuts. One of the two evening seatings requires reservations, and service may be hurried. However, after tasting the house-made pear cake with ginger, these drawbacks will be hard to ignore.

4. Knowledge of the East

Owner Hamed Ahmadi arrived in Venice as a refugee in 2006, and his restaurants depend on his experience as well as that of his workers, who also came by the same road from all over the globe. The first restaurant in Cannaregio was so successful that he created a second one in Dorsoduro. There are options like Afghan ravioli with a spicy chickpea sauce, Pakistani cream chicken with apple, and Greek-style vegetables with yogurt on the menu, which is a wonderful blend of foods from their home countries and those they traveled through on the way to Italy. Since everything is prepared in preparation and is served canteen-style, the enormous platters—from which you can choose up to five dishes—are astonishingly affordable and the service is lightning-quick.

5. Quadri's Restaurant

Since it opened as Gran Caffè Quadri in 1775, the restaurant located above the café has been a staple of St. Mark's Square. It is now owned and operated by the Michelin-starred Alajmo brothers from the neighborhood, and designer and architect Philippe Starck gave it a makeover. Murano glass chandeliers provide a lively and extremely unique glow over walls covered in textiles created by regional textile designers. It would be enough to visit just to see these lavish dining rooms with views of St. Mark's Square, but the five- or eight-course tasting menus that are seasonally inspired are the real draw. With every bite of vegetables from the lagoon island of Sant'Erasmo or tarragon risotto with pepper and mango sauce, you will taste a little bit of spring. Generous amuse-bouches are amusing and delectable as well. One of the few Venice menus that offer gluten-free alternatives is this one.

6. Antiche Carampane

The Bortoluzzi family, whose popular restaurant is tucked away in San Polo's maze, is happy to impart culinary customs handed down through the decades; owner Piera's father was a fish merchant at the Rialto market. The daily catch from the Rialto, expertly sliced and served raw, carpaccio di pesce crudo, baccalà mantecato (creamed salt cod), and big seafood platters that are perfectly battered and fried showcase the chef's passion for high-quality, fresh ingredients. This is traditional Venetian cuisine served at the finest level (frequently to visiting celebrities like Bill Murray and Yoko Ono), so don't expect pizza or lasagna. Bookings are required.

7. Oke

It would be kind to say that Venice isn't renowned for its pizza, but Oke defies the mold and also offers some of the nicest views in town. There is conventional seating inside, but for a slight surcharge, you can dine outdoors, right on the renowned Zattere coastline, with the Giudecca canal lapping at your feet and passing boats while you slice your crust. The pizza is excellent; you may get it with whole, Khorasan wheat, spelled, or gluten-free bases, and you can select from a variety of premium Italian toppings, such as handmade sopressa salami and caramelized Tropea onions. Both the veggies and some of the flour are all organic. Their enormous salads are perfect for the summer heat, and everything is also quite reasonably priced.

8. Taverna La Fenice

Having a restaurant that specializes in meat in this city known for its seafood seems extremely un-Venetian. However, this location, hidden behind the Fenice opera building, is among the most eerie in the city, with its swirling glass windows transporting you to an age of art nouveau. Maria Callas and other opera legends have long gathered here after performances; now, it serves as a calm, elegant hideaway from the city's congested streets. Don't miss their specialty dish, the *Risotto Secoe*, which has delicate pork slices that melt into the rice.

9. Venissa

The trek to Mazzorbo Island in the north lagoon makes up about half of the Venissa adventure. This Michelin-starred restaurant pays homage to the lagoon's past by using fish obtained in nearby Burano and a lot of vegetables produced in the garden out back. This is where Venice first emerged. The seven- or ten-course tasting menus include dishes like turbot with potatoes, porcini mushrooms, black summer truffle, bay leaves or smoked eel, beetroot, kombucha, and sorrel. A tight budget? The cuisine at the more relaxed Osteria Venissa, also on the property, is made in the same kitchen.

10. Al Covo

Al Covo is one of those tried-and-true favorites with a menu that leans more toward regional cuisines from Veneto and the city of Venice. Al Covo is a small, rustic restaurant with some outside seating on nicer days. It has been owned by the same family since 1987, notably by a married pair made up of a local Florentine and a native Texan. With a concentration of fish from nearby waterways, the servings are substantial, fresh, and exquisitely presented. Examples include linguini with nearby clams and Adriatic monkfish wrapped in crispy pancetta and served with celeriac fondue and Giàlet beans.

11. Eolo

You need time to begin understanding Venice correctly, which includes time to learn about its cuisine. There is no better way to appreciate the lagoon and everything it has to offer if you have the time to try something new than with a culinary "cruise" on Eolo. This is not your typical tour, however; Eolo is a classic bragozzo, a flat-bottomed wooden sailing boat ideal for the lagoon's sheltered waters. Mauro Stoppa, the restaurant's chef, owner, and captain, is an adept navigator who is familiar with the lagoon's canals, channels, and the traditional and age-old dishes he makes for customers. You'll purchase freshly caught fish from a local fisherman from boat to boat, and Mauro will add veggies he's grown himself on a lagoon island, as well as wild herbs collected from the barene (mudflats). Instead of dining at a restaurant, a cruise is an exquisite day out that includes a five-course dinner that is made aboard. Cruises are at least one full day long.

12. Terrazza Danieli

Excellent cuisine is served at this rooftop restaurant atop the famous Hotel Danieli. The menu features dishes from the 19th century, such as the Dandolo risotto from 1909, which includes sea urchin, sole, and fresh tomatoes. This location offers one of the nicest views in all of Venice, with a vista of the Grand Canal, Punta della Dogana, Giudecca, and San Giorgio

Maggiore. However, that is really beside the point.

13. Enoteca Al Volto

This wine bar has been enchanting residents and visitors alike since 1936 with courteous service, substantial Venetian food, and traditional cicchetti bar snacks. Look for the wooden table on Calle Cavalli, not far from Rialto Bridge, to explore old-world Venice, where antique wine labels line the bar ceiling and wood paneling decorates a cozy dining area. The pricing is fair, particularly by Venice standards, and reservations are required. The servings are very big. Affordable house wines go well with traditional dishes like spaghetti with clams and Venetian-style liver with polenta.

14. Santa Marina's Osteria

This outstanding restaurant specializes in raw fish dishes, such as open squid filled with tuna tartar and scallop carpaccio. But don't overlook the main courses, such as the amazing plate of fried fish, or the pasta (try the spaghettoni with duck). L'Osteria di Santa Marina was once a sandwich shop, like many renowned Italian eateries, but Chef Agostino Doria has since turned it into a culinary institution in the area. The a la carte menu is available, or you may pick the tasting menu and leave it up to the culinary gods. On balmy evenings, sit outdoors to enjoy views of the campo (square), but if it's a bit chilly outside, the interiors are just as cozy. Even if the service might be a little abrasive, this is traditional Venetian cuisine with a modern touch.

CONCLUSION

Venice is an amazing city. It attracts tourists with the splendor of its architecture, canals, and the artwork it displays in its churches and galleries. It charms with its exquisite cuisine and drinks, as well as with its brilliant artisans who use leather and glass to create works of art.

The Venetian Lagoon is home to hundreds of islands, making it difficult to travel by anything other than foot or boat. Due to the lack of motorized traffic, Venice has a calm ambiance that lets tourists concentrate on taking in the sights and flavors of the city.

With its cozy gondolas and exquisite artwork, Venice is a place for lovers. But it goes beyond that. It is a city for all people. Venice is a city you will admire whether you have an interest in the arts, movies, music, or architecture, or if you just wish to be enchanted by a magnificent location.

Printed in Great Britain
by Amazon